Passing Your Driving Test in Ireland

The Essential Guide

PASSING YOUR DRIVING TEST IN IRELAND

THE ESSENTIAL GUIDE

Noel Byrnes

ORPEN PRESS

Published by
Orpen Press
Lonsdale House
Avoca Avenue
Blackrock
Co. Dublin
Ireland

email: info@orpenpress.com
www.orpenpress.com

© Noel Byrnes, 2012
© Diagrams, Orpen Press, 2012

ISBN 978-1-871305-56-2

A catalogue record for this book is available from the British Library. All rights reserved. No part of this publication may be reproduced, stored in a retrieval system or transmitted in any form or by any means, electronic, mechanical, photocopying, recording or otherwise, without the prior, written permission of the publisher.
This book is sold subject to the condition that it shall not, by way of trade or otherwise, be lent, resold, hired out, or otherwise circulated without the publisher's prior consent in any form of binding or cover other than that in which it is published and without a similar condition including this condition being imposed on the subsequent purchaser.

Printed in Slovenia by Almarose, d.o.o.'
Layout and diagrams by Susan Waine

*Dedicated to my parents Mary and Terence Byrnes,
my siblings Mary, Ger, Margaret, Dianne and Evelyn, Uncle Billy
and my wife Marcella.
To our two beautiful children, Matthew and Terri, we wish you health,
happiness and success as you both make your way in life,
making this world an even more amazing place.*

About the Author

Noel Byrnes is an approved driving instructor (ADI) currently registered with the Road Safety Authority (RSA). He has worked for several years as a driving instructor, taking learner drivers from the absolute basics to passing the driving test and beyond with advanced driving courses. Over the years his experience has given him an excellent insight into the issues facing the learner driver and the challenges which are faced when it comes to passing the test. For this reason he decided to write this guide to explain in detail what the driver tester is looking for and so give the learner driver a step-by-step guide to passing the test.

Acknowledgements

This first edition of *Passing Your Driving Test in Ireland: The Essential Guide* would not have been possible without Mr Dan Bindman's advice and editorial assistance. Thank you. Road sign images were sourced from the Rules of the Road.

Disclaimer

While every care has been taken in the production of this book, no legal responsibility is accepted, warranted or implied by the author, editor or publisher in respect of any errors, omissions or mis-statements. You should use this book in conjunction with driving lessons from an RSA approved driving instructor.

How to Use this Guide

This guide was written with the purpose of providing the new learner driver with all the necessary information needed to pass the practical car driving test in Ireland. It also aims to provide an understanding of recent changes in legislation which affect the process of becoming a fully qualified driver in Ireland.

Information is provided on how to choose an approved driving instructor (ADI) and the documentation you need to have in your possession before you are allowed to sit your test. It also incorporates information on the Essential Driver Training (EDT) syllabus, which was introduced on 4 April 2011.

To complement this guide and aid clarity simple illustrations of driving manoeuvres are also included.

To finally demystify the practical driving test, the actual driver tester's report form is included and broken down into detailed explanations. This means that you will know exactly what the driver tester is expecting from your driving.

Using this guide combined with lessons from an ADI will hugely increase your success rate.

Contents

1. **How to Choose Your Driving Instructor** — 1
2. **Understanding the Graduated Driving Licensing System** — 3
   - Your EDT Logbook — 4
3. **Step-by-Step Guide to the Practical Driving Test** — 6
   - Stage 1: At the Driving Test Centre Office — 6
   - Stage 2: Checks at Your Vehicle — 7
   - Stage 3: In Your Vehicle and on the Road with the Tester — 8
   - Stage 4: Return to the Test Centre Office — 10
4. **Essential Documentation and Preparation of Your Vehicle for Your Driving Test** — 11
   - Essential Documentation — 11
   - Essential Vehicle Preparation — 11
5. **Driver Tester's Report Form and Marking Guidelines** — 14
   - Tester's Report Form — 14
   - Tester's Marking Guidelines — 15
   - Understanding the Marking System — 15
6. **Step-by-Step Breakdown of Tester's Report Form (Top Tips Included)** — 18
   - Rules/Checks — 18
   - Position — 19
   - Observation — 24

Contents

♦ Reaction to Hazards	26
♦ Mirrors	28
♦ Clearance/Overtaking	29
♦ Signals	30
♦ Motorcycles	33
♦ Courtesy	33
♦ Alighting	34
♦ Progress	34
♦ Vehicle Controls	36
♦ Speed	39
♦ Traffic Controls	40
♦ Right of Way	42
♦ Reverse	44
♦ Turnabout	46
♦ Parking	48
7. **Sample Questions with Answers**	50
♦ Questions	50
♦ Answers	53
8. **The Essential Top Ten Checklist to Pass the Test**	58
♦ Confirm Test Appointment	58
♦ Permit	58
♦ EDT Logbook	58
♦ Vehicle	58
♦ Vehicle Discs	58
♦ Rules of the Road	58
♦ Under the Bonnet Checks	58

- ♦ Vehicle Secondary Controls ... 58
- ♦ Route Knowledge ... 58
- ♦ Regulation 'L' Plates ... 58

9. **How to Apply for Your Theory and Practical Driving Tests** ... 60
   - ♦ Booking Your Theory Test ... 60
   - ♦ Booking Your Practical Test ... 61

10. **Illustrations of Vehicle Positions and Manoeuvres** ... 62
    - ♦ Driving on the Straight ... 62
    - ♦ Turning Left ... 62
    - ♦ Turning Right ... 62
    - ♦ Emerging at Junctions ... 62
    - ♦ Roundabouts ... 62
    - ♦ Hand Signals for Other Road Users Behind You ... 63
    - ♦ Hand Signals for a Pointsman ... 63
    - ♦ Zebra Crossings ... 63
    - ♦ Yellow Box Junctions ... 63
    - ♦ Stationary Vehicles ... 64
    - ♦ Turnabout Manoeuvre ... 64
    - ♦ Reverse ... 64
    - ♦ Stopping Distances ... 64

11. **Irish Road Signs** ... 65
    - ♦ Regulatory Traffic Signs ... 65
    - ♦ Mandatory Signs at Junctions ... 66
    - ♦ Bus/Tram/Cycle Lanes ... 67
    - ♦ Traffic Lane Control Signs in a Tunnel ... 67
    - ♦ Warning Traffic Signs ... 68

Contents

- ♦ General Purpose Warning Signs — 69
- ♦ Warning Signs for Schools and Children — 71
- ♦ Warning Signs for Road Works — 71
- ♦ Motorway Signs — 74
- ♦ Information Signs — 75
- ♦ Tourist Information Signs — 76

Useful Websites — 77
Glossary of Frequently Used Terms — 78

How to Choose a Driving Instructor

Since 1 May 2009 all driving instructors in Ireland have to be registered with the Road Safety Authority (RSA). In order to become an approved driving instructor (ADI) a three-part instructor's examination has to be passed. In addition to this, each instructor must pass Garda vetting and be tax compliant.

As choosing your instructor is one of the most important decisions you will make it is essential to know that your instructor is approved and registered with the RSA. Please see the tips below to help you choose the right instructor for you.

Top Tips

- Confirm that your instructor is an ADI registered with the RSA. Ask to see their ID issued by the RSA.
- Use recommendations from friends, family and work colleagues.
- Ask about the suitability of the driving school vehicle. Is it fitted with dual controls?
- Does the ADI provide a door-to-door service?
- Is your ADI registered to provide the Essential Driver Training (EDT) syllabus?

Ensure that your ADI's training schedule will fit yours. For example, if you can only take lessons at weekends make sure that your chosen ADI works weekends.

Understanding the Graduated Driving Licensing System 2

If you received your first learner permit on or after 4 April 2011 you are required to complete the Essential Driver Training (EDT) programme. This is basically a programme of staged learning and licensing where the privilege of being allowed to drive on the road is acquired through a structured experience over a period of time. This consists of completing twelve EDT lessons (each lesson being one hour in duration). In addition to this, the 'six-month rule' applies, which means that you must have held your first learner permit for a minimum of six months before you are allowed to sit your practical driving test. Learner drivers will not be able to obtain a driving test date until the RSA has received confirmation from the learner driver's ADI that the twelve EDT lessons have been completed. Learner drivers can now check their own lesson records by going to www.rsa.ie and using their licence number and personal details to sign in to the 'My EDT' link.

Your ADI will bring you through each of your EDT lessons in detail:

- ♦ Lesson 1: Car controls and safety checks
- ♦ Lesson 2: Correct positioning

Passing Your Driving Test in Ireland

Learner Permit issued before 4 April 2011

[Theory test] → [Practical driving test] → [Repeat test until you pass]

Learner Permit issued on or after 4 April 2011

[Theory test] → [12 EDT lessons Hold permit for 6 months] → [Practical driving test] → [Repeat test until you pass]

- ♦ Lesson 3: Changing direction
- ♦ Lesson 4: Progression management
- ♦ Lesson 5: Correct positioning
- ♦ Lesson 6: Anticipation and reaction
- ♦ Lesson 7: Sharing the road
- ♦ Lesson 8: Driving safely through traffic
- ♦ Lesson 9: Changing direction (more complex situations)
- ♦ Lesson 10: Speed management
- ♦ Lesson 11: Driving calmly
- ♦ Lesson 12: Night driving

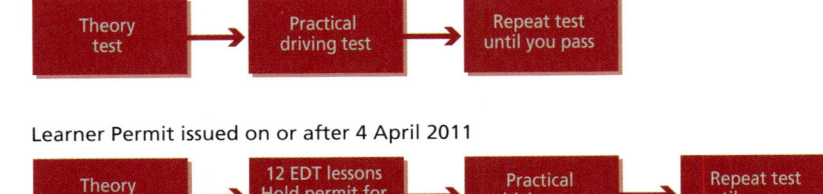

Your EDT Logbook

At the end of each EDT lesson your instructor will fill in and stamp your logbook, which must also be signed by both the learner and the instructor. This is a vital course to complete in order to be safe on the road and to be allowed to actually sit your driving test. Keep your logbook carefully in a secure location. (See examples on next page.)

Understanding the Graduated Driving Licensing System

PRE LESSON CHECKS

Approved Driving Instructor

The following checks must be carried out before each EDT lesson. Both learner and ADI must confirm that the checks have been completed before the lesson, and sign the Declaration in the relevant column below.

CHECKS

1. Items	2. Details	3. Methodology
Identity Check	ADI must satisfy him / herself as to the identity of the person attending for training.	Identify the person from the learner permit photograph.
Documentation is in Order	Learner Permit. Insurance cover. Tax Disc.	Check learner permit licence category as well as commencement (ó/from) and expiry (go/to) dates. Record learners 'Driver Number' and Date of Birth in the Logbook. Check insurance disc is in order. Check that a valid tax disc is on display. Check that NCT disc is on display (if applicable).
Fitness to Drive	Check that the learner is in a fit condition to drive and take the lesson.	Learner to confirm that they are fit and not under the influence of alcohol or drugs that may affect their capabilities. Check that (if applicable) the learner is wearing corrective lenses.
Roadworthiness of Vehicle	Check that the vehicle to be used for the lesson is suitable for use.	Check that the vehicle meets learner permit category. Carry out routine vehicle checks to ensure the vehicle is roadworthy; tyres, lights, glass, bodywork, mirrors, reflectors, number plates, wheels, etc. Check that 'L' plates are fitted.

These checks should be carried out for each lesson whether an ADI vehicle is used or not. Where the vehicle is provided by the Learner enter Learner in the relevant column. If the vehicle used is a provided by the driving instructor then enter ADI in the column.

DECLARATION

Lesson	Vehicle Provider	Learner Signature	ADI Signature	Lesson	Vehicle Provider	Learner Signature	ADI Signature
1				7			
2				8			
3				9			
4				10			
5				11			
6				12			

ESSENTIAL DRIVER TRAINING

Approved Driving Instructor

M _____ Date of Birth: ___ / ___ / ___ Driver number: ___ / _____

This confirms the completion of EDT Lesson 1 relating to Car Controls and Safety Checks. The minimum content for the lesson has been delivered and in the Feedback section below I have described the learner's progress towards meeting the expected outcomes. The objectives and expected outcomes for this lesson are described in the EDT Syllabus which is available in the Essential Driver Training Learner Information Booklet and online at www.rsa.ie

ADI Feedback:

Recommended Actions:

Signed (ADI) _____ Date of Issue: / /
Print Name (ADI) _____ Stamp:
ADI Number _____
Learner Signature _____

Please keep your Logbook in a safe place. Take time to reflect on your ADIs comments as well as your self analysis. Take it along to each practice session with your Sponsor and ask them to make notes to help you. Your ADI may wish to review your Logbook to help in planning your next lesson and your driver tester may need to record it on the day of your driving test.

5

3 Step-by-Step Guide to the Practical Driving Test

This is a step-by-step guide to the practical driving test. It explains what will happen in detail and the sequence in which it takes place on the day of your test. To keep things simple I have broken the practical test down into four stages as listed below:

- **Stage 1:** At the tester's desk in the test centre
- **Stage 2:** At your vehicle for your vehicle checks
- **Stage 3:** The actual driving of your vehicle on the test route
- **Stage 4:** Back at the test centre office for your result

Stage 1: At the Driving Test Centre Office

- Present yourself at your designated test centre at least fifteen minutes before your test is due to start.
- You will be greeted by your assigned driver tester and shown to his/her desk. The driver tester will request your address and ask for your vehicle make and model details. On occasion, a supervising examiner may accompany your driver tester on the test. The purpose of this is to ensure that your driver tester conducts the test in a fair and correct manner.
- If you received your first learner permit on or after 4 April 2011 you will have to provide your stamped and completed

EDT logbook to your driver tester prior to commencing your test.
- The driver tester will check to make sure your permit is valid (e.g. valid dates and correct category of vehicle).
- You will be asked to sign and date a statement confirming the roadworthy condition and insurance status of your vehicle.
- You will then be asked questions on the rules of the road. Testers are required to ask questions in relation to pedestrian crossings, headlights, right of way, traffic lights and road signs. Further questions regarding other aspects of the rules of the road may also be asked. See Chapter 7 for sample questions and answers.

Stage 2: Checks at Your Vehicle

- The tester will check that 'L' plates are displayed to the front and rear of the vehicle.
- Your insurance disc, tax disc and National Car Test (NCT) disc (if required) are checked to ensure they are valid. See Chapter 4 for more details about the NCT.
- The driver tester then notes the registration number on the report sheet.
- If the vehicle has an automatic transmission the driver tester will inform you that on passing the test the issued licence will be restricted to vehicles with an automatic transmission.

- ♦ The driver tester will also check front and rear indicators, brake lights and headlights for their correct operation from outside the vehicle.
- ♦ For the technical checks you will be asked to identify and verbally explain checks on any three of the following:
  - ❑ Tyres
  - ❑ Engine oil
  - ❑ Windscreen washer
  - ❑ Coolant
  - ❑ Reflectors
  - ❑ Steering/power steering fluid
  - ❑ Horn operation
  - ❑ Brakes

Please note that the bonnet will have to be opened, secured and closed again securely to complete some of these tasks. Please note that these checks are done at the tester's discretion.

Stage 3: In Your Vehicle and on the Road with the Tester

Once in the car with the driver tester you will be instructed to begin by the tester saying, 'Please start up the engine. Now before you move off, I want you to show me how you would operate some of the controls.' You will usually be asked to operate three of the following:

- ♦ Rear fog lights
- ♦ Air intake control

- ♦ Temperature control
- ♦ Wipers
- ♦ Dipped headlights
- ♦ Windscreen washer
- ♦ Air vents
- ♦ Rear window heater
- ♦ Air conditioning (if fitted)

Then you will be asked to 'Ensure that the seat, seatbelt, head restraint and mirrors are properly adjusted and that your door is properly closed.' Once this is complete you will be instructed by the driver tester to 'Drive in your normal manner. I will tell you in good time when to turn right or left; otherwise you follow the course of the road. If you have any doubts about my directions ask me to repeat or clarify them. You may start when you are ready.'

In addition to following the driving directions from the driver tester you will also be asked to perform the following manoeuvres as the test progresses:

- ♦ Turnabout manoeuvre
- ♦ Reverse manoeuvre
- ♦ Hand signals
- ♦ Hill test
- ♦ Parking

(Chapter 6 will discuss these practical manoeuvres in detail along with all the other areas of driving required to pass your practical test.)

Stage 4: Return to the Test Centre Office

As your test is coming to an end the driver tester will inform you that 'We are now coming towards the end of your test, please find a suitable place and park.' Once the vehicle is safely parked and the engine turned off the tester will say 'We will now return to the office and I'll give you the result of the test. Thank you.'

In the office at the test centre you will be given a certificate with the result of your driving test.

Essential Documentation and Preparation of Your Vehicle for Your Driving Test

Essential Documentation

- Confirm the time, date and location of your test appointment. Refer to your notification letter, e-mail or text message to ensure you have the correct information.
- Ensure that your permit licence is valid (i.e. that the document has not expired and the vehicle details relate to the correct category of vehicle for which you are being tested) and in your possession.
- If you received your first driving permit on or after 4 April 2011 you will have to produce your stamped and completed EDT logbook to your driver tester before commencing your test.

Essential Vehicle Preparation

- Make sure your vehicle is correctly taxed, insured and has a current NCT disc if required. It is a legal requirement to have car insurance and to tax your car, and to display the relevant discs.

- All cars four years old or older must undergo an NCT test. The NCT due date is calculated by reference to the date of first registration of the car, with tests due every two years for cars registered less than ten years ago.
- An annual NCT test for cars ten years old or older is required from 1 June 2011. This means that all cars presented on their tenth anniversary or subsequent NCT on or after 1 June 2011 will receive a certificate valid for up to one year only. The NCT falls due on the anniversary of the vehicle's first registration. So, if you receive your NCT certificate three months after it falls due your NCT certificate will be valid for either nine months or twenty-one months (depending on the age of your vehicle).

Age of Vehicle	Test Frequency
0–3 years	No test required
4–9 years	Every 2 years
10 years or more	Annually
Cars registered before 1 January 1980	No test required

- Please also ensure that your vehicle is in a roadworthy condition.
- Be thoroughly familiar with the operation of your vehicle's secondary controls. For example, the safe operation of lights, windscreen wipers, screen washer, air conditioning unit, heater controls, horn and demisters.

- Be skilled in opening, securing and closing the bonnet of your vehicle. The examiner may ask you to point to items such as the containers for brake fluid, coolant, windscreen washer fluid and power steering fluid (if fitted) and also to explain how to check the oil level of your engine. Remember that you are only required to show and tell the driver tester the engine components. Do not touch or place your hands on the engine or in the engine bay area as you will risk injury.
- Be capable of answering questions in relation to tyre checks, vehicle warning signs (e.g. the oil light) and how to recognise signs of brake or steering defects. The examiner may also refer to these items when doing the vehicle checks.

5 Driver Tester's Report Form and Marking Guidelines

No. 000000

DRIVING TEST REPORT

RSA

1. Passed your Driving Test

Having passed your driving test you should nevertheless continue to pay particular attention to the faults marked overleaf without neglecting other aspects of your driving.

2. Failure of your Driving Test

Failure of the test arises where you incur any of the following:

1 or more grade 3 faults;

4 of the same grade 2 faults for a single aspect;

6 or more grade 2 faults under the same heading; or a total of

9 or more grade 2 faults overall.

Up to a maximum of 4 grade 2 faults may be recorded for any single aspect.

3. Grading of faults

Faults are graded as follows:

Grade 1 (Green Area) Minor Fault, Grade 2 (Blue Area) More Serious Fault, Grade 3 (Pink Area) Dangerous/Potentially Dangerous faults or total disregard of traffic controls.

Grade 1 faults do not affect the rest result.

A combination of 3 or more unanswered or incorrectly answered questions on the Rules of the Road/ Checks, constitutes a grade 2 fault. (Checks include doors closed safely, the headrest, mirrors, seat and seat-belt adjustments, and for motorcyclists, the helmet, gloves, boots and protective clothing).

3 or more hand signals not demonstrated correctly constitutes a grade 2 fault.

3 or more Secondary Controls not demonstrated correctly constitutes a grade 2 fault. (Secondary controls include temperature controls, fan, air vents, rear-window heater, wipers, windscreen washer, light switches, air intake control, rear fog light and air conditioner, if fitted).

Not operating a Secondary Control as required during the practical test can also constitute a fault.

4. Technical Checks – all categories

Inability to describe a check on 3 or more of the following constitutes a grade 2 fault:

The tyres, lights, reflectors, indicators, engine oil, coolant, windscreen washer fluid, steering, brakes and horn. Where necessary, the bonnet should be opened and closed safely. For motorcyclists the checks can also include the chain, and the emergency stop-switch, if fitted.

For categories C1, C, D1, D, EC1, ED1, and ED technical checks include the following as appropriate to the category:

The power assisted braking and steering systems, the condition of the wheels, wheel nuts, mudguards, windscreen, windows, wipers, air-pressure, air tanks, suspension, engine oil, coolant, windscreen washer fluid, the loading mechanism if fitted, the body, sheets, cargo doors, cabin locking, way of loading and securing the load, and checking and using the instrument panel and tachograph.

For categories D1, D, ED1 and ED technical checks include controlling the body, service doors, emergency exits, first aid equipment, fire extinguishers and other safety equipment.

5. Coupling/Uncoupling includes

a) Checking the coupling mechanism and the brake and electrical connections,

b) Uncoupling and recoupling the trailer from/to its towing vehicle using the correct sequence. The towing vehicle must be parked alongside the trailer as part of the exercise.

Parking in relation to categories EB, C1, C, EC1, and EC includes parking safely at a ramp or platform for loading/unloading.

Parking in relation to D1, D, ED1, and ED includes parking safely to let passengers on or off the bus.

6. Motorcyclists

Safety glance means looking around to check blind spots as necessary.

7. Preparing for your next Driving Test

In Preparing for your next test you should pay particular attention to the items which have been marked. Further information on these and other aspects of the test are contained in the booklet entitled "Rules of the Road" which is available at book shops and in the leaflet "Preparing for your Driving Test" which is issued with the acknowledgement of your application.

8. Note

Items on which faults occurred during your driving test are marked overleaf. The driver tester is not permitted to discuss the details of the test.

Driver Tester's Report Form and Marking Guidelines

Faults	Grade 1	Grade 2	Grade 3	Faults	Grade 1	Grade 2	Grade 3
1. RULES/CHECKS				**11. PROGRESS**	Maintain reasonable progress and avoid undue hesitancy when		
2. POSITION	Position vehicle correctly and in good time						
On the Straight				Moving Off			
On Bends				On the Straight			
In Traffic Lanes				Overtaking			
At Cross Junctions				At Cross Junctions			
At Roundabouts				At Roundabouts			
Turning Right				Turning Right			
Turning Left				Turning Left			
Stopping				Changing Lanes			
Following Traffic				At Traffic Lights			
3. OBSERVATION	take proper observation			**12. VEHICLE CONTROLS**	Make proper use of		
Moving Off				Accelerator			
Overtaking				Clutch			
Changing Lane				Gears			
At Cross Junctions				Footbrake			
At Roundabouts				Handbrake			
Turning Right				Steering			
Turning Left				Secondary Controls			
4. REACT TO HAZARDS	React promptly and properly to hazards			Technical Checks			
Reaction				Coupling/Uncoupling			
5. MIRRORS	Use properly, in good time and before signalling			**13. SPEED**	Adjust speed to suit/on approach		
Moving Off				Road Conditions			
On the Straight				Traffic Conditions			
Overtaking				Roundabouts			
Changing Lanes				Cross Junctions			
At Roundabouts				Turning Right			
Turning Right				Turning Left			
Turning Left				Traffic Controls			
Slowing/Stopping				Speed Limit			
6. CLEARANCE/OVERTAKING	Allow sufficient clearance to			**14. TRAFFIC CONTROLS**	Comply with		
Pedestrians				Traffic Lights			
Cyclists				Traffic Signs			
Stationary Vehicles				Road Markings			
Other Traffic				Pedestrian Crossing			
Other Objects				Garda/School Warden			
Overtake Safely				Bus Lanes			
7. SIGNALS	Give correct signal in good time			Cycle Lanes			
Moving Off				**15. RIGHT OF WAY**	Yield right of way as required		
Overtaking				Moving Off			
Changing Lane				Overtaking			
At Roundabouts				Changing Lanes			
Turning Right				At Junctions			
Turning Left				At Roundabouts			
Stopping				Turning Right			
Cancel Promptly				Turning Left			
Hand Signals				**16. REVERSE**			
Do not beckon others				Competently			
Misleading				Observation			
8. MOTORCYCLES				Right of Way			
Safety Glance				**17. TURNABOUT**			
U-Turn/Control/Obs/Yld				Competently			
Slow Ride Controls/Obs				Observation			
Park On/Off Stand				Right of Way			
Walk Alongside				**18. PARKING**	Loading/Unloading/Passenger stops		
				Competently			
9. COURTESY				Right of Way			
10. ALIGHTING				Legally			

Understanding the Marking System

As you can see, the driver tester's report sheet is broken into eighteen main headings and then colour-coded into sections of green, blue and pink. The shaded grey area is not applicable at this time. Please refer to the tester's report sheet combined with the explanations below to best understand the marking system.

Grading of Faults

- Grade 1 Faults (green area): These are minor faults and do not affect the test result. For example, being unable to answer or incorrectly answering a single question on the rules of the road and/or checks may give you a single grade 1 (green) fault. We will not discuss these below as they do not affect your chances of passing your test.
- Grade 2 Faults (blue area): These are more serious faults and do affect the test result. For example, being unable to answer three or more questions or answering them incorrectly may constitute a grade 2 (blue) fault. Another example may be incorrect positioning on a left-hand corner.
- Grade 3 Faults (pink area): These are seen as dangerous or potentially dangerous faults. For example, not stopping at a stop sign/marking or not reacting promptly and properly to a hazard may constitute a grade 3 (pink) fault.

How Many Mistakes Will Mean Failure of the Driving Test?

Grade 2 Faults (Blue Area)

- Four grade 2 (blue) mistakes for the same aspect of your driving will result in the failure of your driving test. In other words, four boxes marked in a row will mean failure of your test. For example, if you choose the incorrect gear four times the four blue boxes on the 'Gear' line under the heading '12. Vehicle Controls' of the driving test report sheet will be marked.

- Six or more grade 2 (blue) faults under the same heading will also result in the failure of your driving test. For example, three grade 2 faults on the 'Overtaking' line and three grade 2 faults on the 'Moving Off' line adds to six grade 2 faults under the same heading ('3. Observation'), which will result in failure of your test.
- Nine or more grade 2 (blue) faults overall will also result in failure of the test.

Grade 3 Faults (Pink Area)

- One or more grade 3 (pink) faults will also result in failure of the test. For example, dangerous or potentially dangerous use of speed while reversing around a corner may result in a grade 3 (pink) fault being recorded.

6 Step-by-Step Breakdown of Tester's Report Form
(Top Tips Included)

1. Rules/Checks

This part of your test is concerned with your vehicle checks and you will also be verbally questioned on your knowledge of the rules of the road and road signs. Sample questions with answers can be found in Chapter 7.

Top Tips

- ♦ Ensure that your permit licence is valid (i.e. the document dates have not expired and vehicle details relate to the correct category of vehicle for which you are being tested) and in your possession.
- ♦ If you received your first driving permit on or after 4 April 2011 you will have to produce your stamped and completed EDT logbook to your driver tester prior to commencing your test.
- ♦ Make sure your vehicle is correctly taxed, insured and has a current NCT disc if required. Please also ensure that your vehicle is in a roadworthy condition.
- ♦ Be thoroughly familiar with the operation of your vehicle's secondary controls. For example, the safe operation of

lights, windscreen wipers, screen washer, air conditioning unit, heater controls, horn and demisters.
- Be skilled in opening the bonnet of your vehicle. The examiner may ask you to point out items such as the containers for brake fluid, coolant, windscreen washer fluid and power steering fluid (if fitted), and also to explain how to check the oil level of your engine.
- Be capable of answering questions in relation to tyre checks, vehicle warning signs (e.g. the oil light) and how to recognise signs of brake or steering defects. The examiner may refer to these items when doing the vehicle checks.

2. Position

- The position of the vehicle will be observed on the straight, on bends, in traffic lanes, at junctions, on roundabouts, turning right and left, stopping and following in traffic. You are required to position your vehicle correctly and in good time. You will also need to have your vehicle positioned correctly in relation to other vehicles and other road users.
- It is also essential to understand that the driver tester is looking to see the correct procedure being used when actually changing from one position to another. This is particularly important when you are turning right or left, dealing with roundabouts and changing lanes. The standard procedure for this is to use the Mirror–Signal–Mirror–Manoeuvre (MSMM) routine.

Passing Your Driving Test in Ireland

Position on the Straight

Top Tips

♦ The vehicle should normally be closer to the left-hand side of the road than to the central dividing line when driving on the straight or on bends.

♦ **Turning right from a major to a minor road:** using the MSMM routine take up your position just to the left of the central dividing line (or where one should normally be if not present) and then make your turn around the central point of the road you are turning into. Avoid cutting the corner. Once you have safely completed the

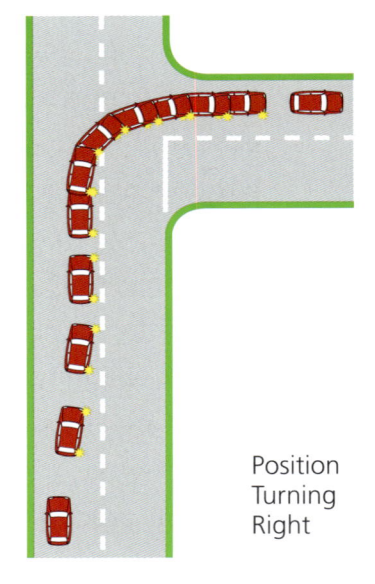

Position Turning Right

Step-by-Step Breakdown of Tester's Report Form

turn, have a quick check in your mirrors and proceed on once the way is safe.

- **Turning right from a minor road to a major road:** using the MSMM routine take up your position just to the left of the central dividing line. You must also obey any road signs or road markings present (norm-

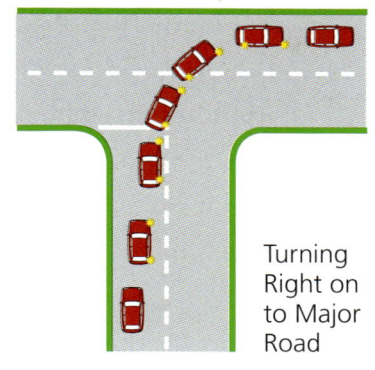

Turning Right on to Major Road

ally a stop or yield sign will be present). You may then creep slowly forward and proceed when the way is safe. Once you have safely completed the turn, have a quick check in your mirrors and proceed on once the way is safe.

- **Turning left from a major to a minor road:** using the MSMM routine approach a left-hand turn as close to the left as is feasible. This position should be maintained during and after your exit from the turn. Once you have safely completed the turn, have a quick check in your mirrors and proceed on once the way is safe.

Position Turning Left

- **Turning left from a minor**

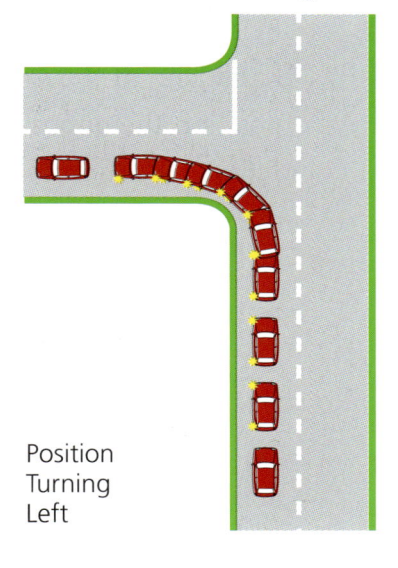

21

to a major road: using your MSMM routine approach a left-hand turn as close to the left as is feasible. Remember that because you are going to enter a major road you will also have to position yourself

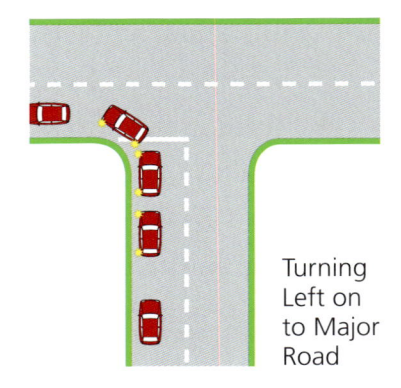

Turning Left on to Major Road

correctly in relation to any regulatory signs at the junction. Typically, this is a stop or yield sign. Once you have safely completed the turn, have a quick check in your mirrors and proceed on once the way is safe.

- ♦ **Rule for correct positioning on roundabouts:** any exit that you are taking on a roundabout that is between the 6 and 12 o'clock position should normally be approached in the left-hand lane. If the exit you are taking is after the 12 o'clock position the approach should be in the right-hand lane. Please note that on occasion road markings may require a different lane to be used and these should be obeyed.
- ♦ **Position on approach to roundabouts:** as you approach a roundabout the driver tester will ask you to take a particular exit off the roundabout. The first thing is to establish where the exit you are taking is in relation to the 12 o'clock rule. The road sign for the roundabout on approach will help you with this. Then using the MSMM

Step-by-Step Breakdown of Tester's Report Form

Roundabout
12 o'clock
Rule

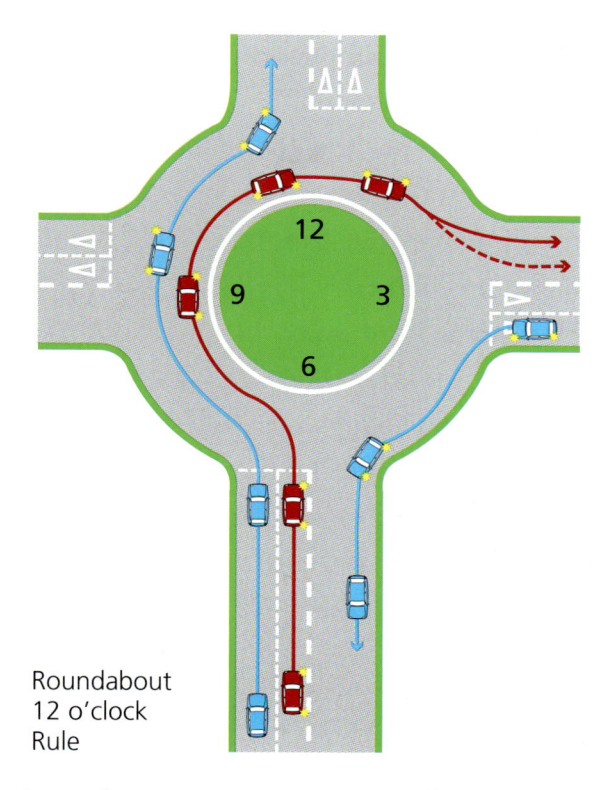

routine take up your position. The signal part of the procedure may be ignored if you do not have to change position on approach.

Positioning at Roundabouts

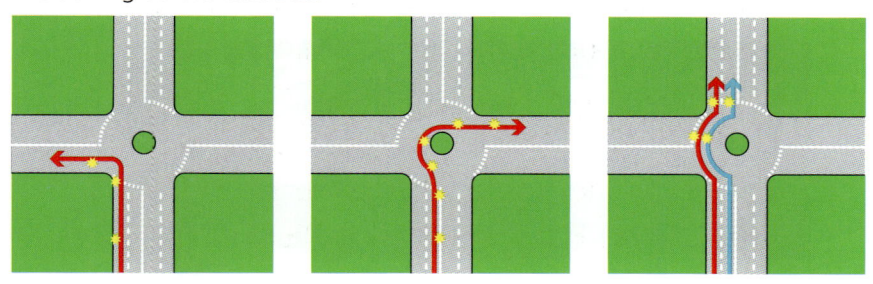

- **Position on the roundabout:** maintain lane discipline while on the roundabout.
- **Position on leaving the roundabout:** as you prepare to leave the roundabout you may again need to change position. Use the MSMM routine and exit the roundabout safely and promptly.
- Changing lanes can be particularly hazardous. Use the MSMM routine, remembering also to check your blind spots before you change position.
- When stopping behind another vehicle make sure that the position is safe and legal and does not delay or obstruct other road users. Make sure you can see the rear tyres of the vehicle in front with a little piece of road surface also being visible.

3. Observation

When using the road you are required to take proper and appropriate observation. Be particularly familiar with what is going on around you when moving off, overtaking, changing lane, at roundabouts and junctions, and turning left and right.

Checking blind spot when moving off

Step-by-Step Breakdown of Tester's Report Form

Blind Spots

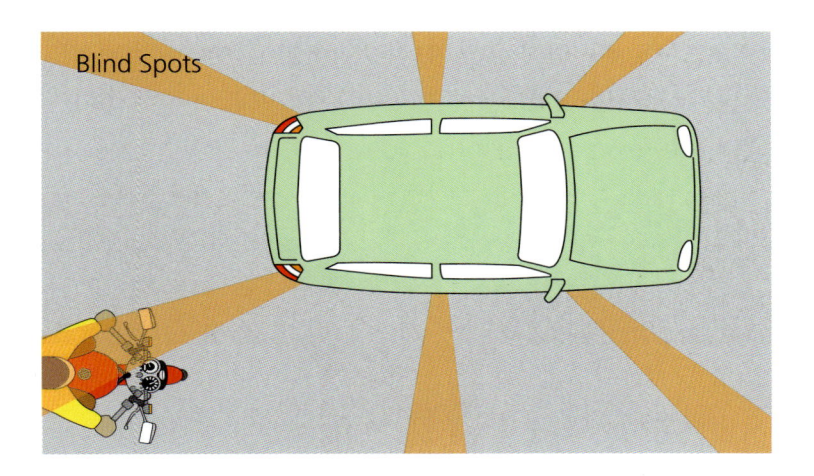

Observation is not simply just looking where you are going. You must look and listen for other potential hazards that may come from any direction.

Top Tips

- ♦ Know your vehicle's blind spots and check those spots accordingly. For example, when you are moving off from a parked position you should check over your right shoulder to get a true picture of what is beside you or to your immediate right as a mirror will not show you this area.
- ♦ Observe where other potential hazards may come from. For example, even if you are going straight ahead at a cross junction you should be aware of what may come from your left and right.
- ♦ When turning right you need to be aware of what may come from your left, and when turning left you need to be aware of what may come from the right.

Passing Your Driving Test in Ireland

♦ It is not enough just to look where you are going. By listening you may hear vehicles coming before they come into view.

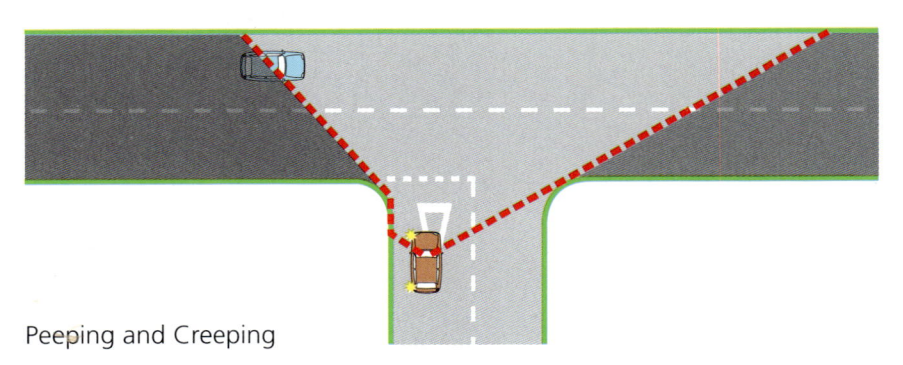

Peeping and Creeping

♦ Where your view is obstructed by walls, ditches, other vehicles or other hazards you must creep slowly forward until you can see clearly if it is safe to proceed. The shaded areas in the illustration above show where walls can block your visibility.

4. Reaction to Hazards

Anticipation combined with prompt and correct responsiveness to hazardous or potentially hazardous situations is an essential part of staying safe on the road.

Top Tips

♦ Pedestrians may be unaware of your presence and may walk behind or in front of your moving vehicle. This may happen frequently in places like car parks where there is

Step-by-Step Breakdown of Tester's Report Form

Hazardous Situation

a mixture of pedestrian and vehicle traffic.
- Be aware that other road users may fail to stop or yield at junctions when they should.
- You need to visually scan for dangers in the near, middle and far distance. This, combined with listening (lower your window if this will help) for other vehicles, may give you vital information to keep you and others safer on the road.
- Understand that there is normally a sequence of events that occur as a hazardous situation develops. For example, if a ball rolls onto the road, expect somebody to follow. Learn to recognise the warning signs.

5. Mirrors

Your mirrors should be used properly and in good time before you use your signal. In other words, the appropriate mirrors should be checked before moving off, stopping, slowing down,

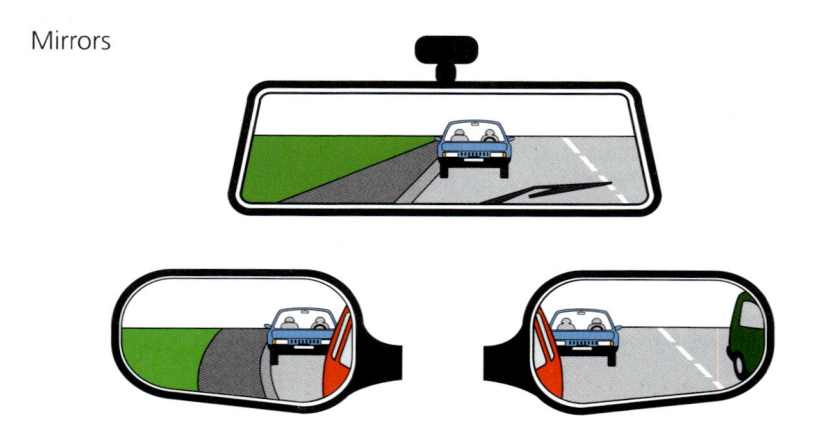

Mirrors

overtaking, changing lanes and turning, and before opening any doors. It is also important that you check your mirrors regularly as you drive.

Top Tips

- Ensure that you know how to adjust your mirrors and that you position them suitably before you move your vehicle.
- Be aware of your blind spots. For example, the driver side wing mirror will not show what is immediately to your right.
- Note that the inside rear view mirror and wing mirrors are made of different types of reflective glass and so may vary in the accuracy of reflecting your surroundings. Objects viewed in the wing mirrors of all vehicles may be closer

Step-by-Step Breakdown of Tester's Report Form

than they appear. Some manufacturers will actually place the warning "objects in the mirror are closer than they appear" on their wing mirrors.

- Mirrors should be used in good time before changing speed or direction. Before you increase or reduce speed you need to be aware of the surrounding situation. You should have a quick glance in your mirrors in the following order: rear view mirror, left wing mirror and then right wing mirror.
- When turning right pay particular attention to your rear view mirror and right wing mirror.
- When turning left pay particular attention to your rear view mirror and left wing mirror.
- Also remember to check your rear view mirror before braking.

6. Clearance/Overtaking

It is essential to allow sufficient but not excessive clearance to other road users and any other obstacles that you may encounter as you use the road. For example, if you are passing a parked vehicle make sure that there is enough room for the vehicle door to open.

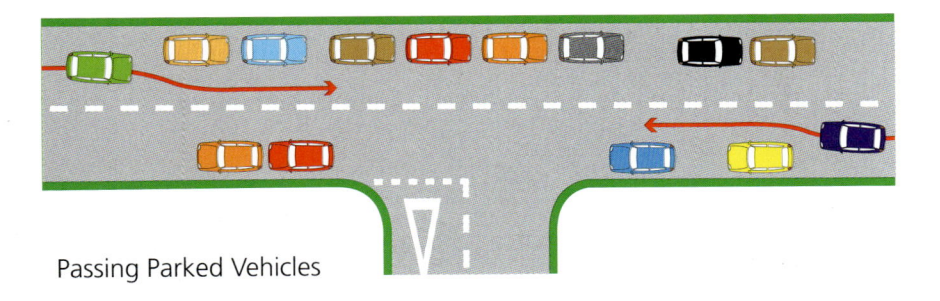

Passing Parked Vehicles

Top Tips

- Before you overtake make sure you have a clear view of the road ahead.
- Make sure it is legal and safe to overtake.
- Use the MSMM (Mirror–Signal–Mirror–Manoeuvre) routine before you overtake and check your mirrors again before returning to the left.
- Give sufficient room to vulnerable road users. For example, a cyclist may lose balance or change road position without warning.

7. Signals

When required, indicators should be used in good time and cancelled promptly when no longer needed. Hand signals will also be examined as part of the driving test.

Top Tips

- When turning left or right allow your indicators to self-correct as you complete the turn and enter the straight section of road. The signal will normally turn off automatically. Sometimes you will have to intervene as the indicators may not self-correct, as on a slight bend.
- If an indicator prematurely switches itself off, simply apply the signal again.
- Avoid signals that may mislead or confuse other road users as this may create a hazardous incident or accident.

Step-by-Step Breakdown of Tester's Report Form

For example, if the driver tester asked you to take the second junction on the right and you signal before you pass the first junction your early signal would give the impression to other road users that you are taking the first junction on the right.

♦ Do not beckon (flash headlights or wave on) other road users during your test as you may invite them into danger. If you are beckoned you may proceed, provided, of course, that it is safe to do so.

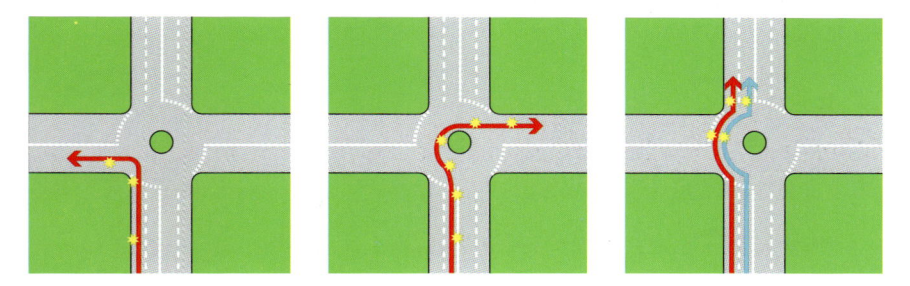

Signalling Approaching a Roundabout

♦ As you approach a roundabout use the 12 o'clock rule to figure out if you need to change position as you approach the roundabout. If you do need to change position use the MSMM routine.
♦ If the first exit you are taking is before the 12 o'clock position you should use the MSMM routine and signal left on approach.
♦ If you are going straight through (the 12 o'clock position) do *not* signal as you approach the roundabout; signal left

31

once you pass the exit before the exit you wish to take.
- If taking an exit *after* the 12 o'clock position signal right as you approach the roundabout, then signal left once you pass the exit before the one you wish to take.
- When preparing to leave the roundabout use the MSMM routine, applying the signal in good time before the exit you are going to use. An example of good time would be applying the signal when you are almost halfway past the exit before the exit you are taking.

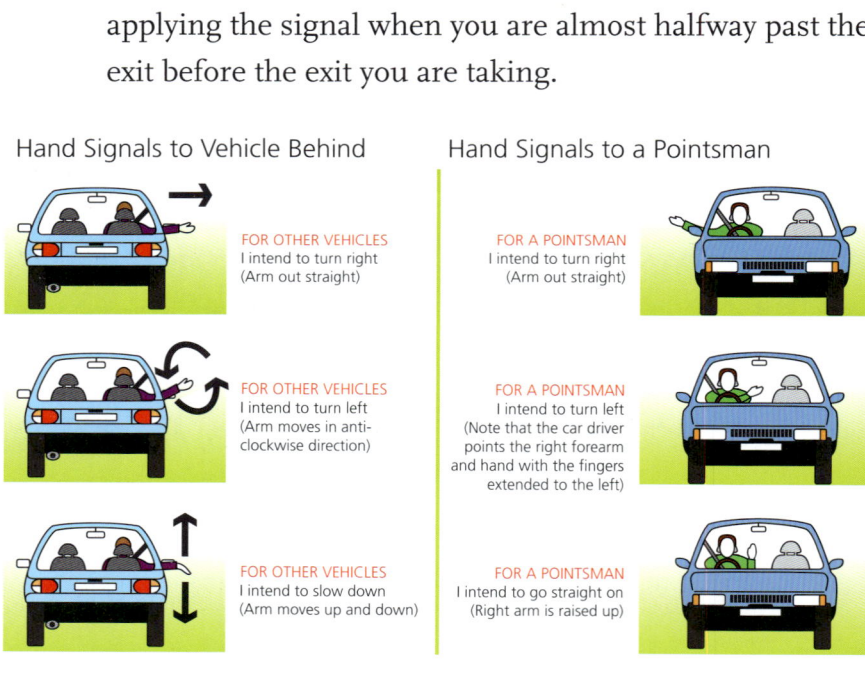

Hand Signals to Vehicle Behind

FOR OTHER VEHICLES
I intend to turn right
(Arm out straight)

FOR OTHER VEHICLES
I intend to turn left
(Arm moves in anti-clockwise direction)

FOR OTHER VEHICLES
I intend to slow down
(Arm moves up and down)

Hand Signals to a Pointsman

FOR A POINTSMAN
I intend to turn right
(Arm out straight)

FOR A POINTSMAN
I intend to turn left
(Note that the car driver points the right forearm and hand with the fingers extended to the left)

FOR A POINTSMAN
I intend to go straight on
(Right arm is raised up)

- You will be asked to demonstrate the hand signals when you are stopped, usually after the turnabout or reverse manoeuvre. There are six hand signals in total. For some of these signals you will be required to open your window.

Be sure to check your blind spots before you place your arm out of the window.

8. Motorcycles

This section of the tester's marking sheet relates to safety, control, slow ride control and u-turn for the motorcycle user. Please contact your local ADI for this category of test and information on the Initial Basic Training (IBT) syllabus.

9. Courtesy

This section is about having road manners. For example, allowing a vehicle from a minor road to merge in front of you into slow-moving traffic. Combine courtesy with care and consideration to make your driving safer and less stressful.

Top Tips

- ♦ Keep a safe distance from the vehicle in front. Avoid tailgating.
- ♦ Before opening your door please make sure it is safe to do so. It is also good practice to advise your passengers of any dangers.
- ♦ When being overtaken by another vehicle avoid increasing speed and slow down if necessary to allow the vehicle to pass.
- ♦ Allow extra room to vulnerable road users.

10. Alighting

Secure your vehicle with your handbrake. Turn the vehicle off and remove the key or card. Be extremely careful when leaving your vehicle. Make proper observation before opening your door as this is where incidents and accidents frequently occur.

Top Tips

- When leaving your vehicle it is also acceptable to have a low gear (first gear for example) engaged. The advantage of this is that in the event of a handbrake malfunction the vehicle will be held in position by the gear. Remember of course to engage neutral gear again before you start your engine.

11. Progress

This topic touches every aspect of your driving. This is where a driver shows experience by avoiding undue hesitancy. An example of good progress would be proceeding at a junction when it is safe to do so. An example of poor progress would be driving at 25 km/h when it is safe and legally permitted to drive up to 50 km/h.

Top Tips

- When stopped behind a vehicle in traffic make sure you can see its rear tyres and a small piece of road surface.
- In normal driving conditions leave a two second gap from the vehicle in front. You can double this distance in wet conditions. This is known as the 'two second rule'.

Step-by-Step Breakdown of Tester's Report Form

Two Second Rule

- To apply the two second rule, pick a point the vehicle in front is passing (for example, a road sign or any other marker). At this point say 'Only a fool breaks the two second rule.' If you are still saying this phrase and you have passed the point you picked you are too close and need to pull back from the vehicle in front.
- When merging with traffic avail of acceptable gaps in the traffic flow. Ask yourself, 'Is it safe to proceed?' If the answer is yes, proceed; if the answer is no, wait. It is difficult to introduce an exact rule as to what is an acceptable gap in the traffic. This is really a judgement call taking into consideration such things as whether you are crossing over a traffic lane, road conditions, visibility and the speed of oncoming traffic. Each situation will differ so it is important that you gain your initial experiences under the supervision of an ADI.

12. Vehicle Controls

Using the vehicle controls (accelerator, clutch, gears, footbrake, handbrake, steering and secondary controls) in the correct manner will result in a smooth, stress-free and safe driving experience for both you and your passengers.

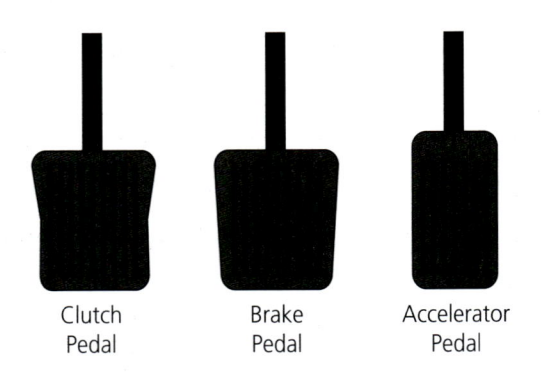

Clutch Pedal   Brake Pedal   Accelerator Pedal

Top Tips

- Use the accelerator pedal as required and avoid using too little (risking the car stalling) or excessive force (excess racing of the engine). For example, moving off uphill needs more acceleration than moving off downhill.
- Change gears smoothly to match the speed at which you are travelling. Ideally you should drive the vehicle in as low a gear as possible while avoiding excessively loud engine noise, but at the same time be in as high a gear as possible while avoiding labouring the vehicle. Here are some guidelines:

Step-by-Step Breakdown of Tester's Report Form

- ❏ First gear for moving off
- ❏ Second gear from 10 km/h to 30 km/h
- ❏ Third gear from 30 km/h to 50 km/h
- ❏ Fourth gear from 50 km/h to 70 km/h
- ❏ Fifth gear from 70 km/h

♦ These are guidelines and may vary depending on the type of vehicle you are driving and the gradient your vehicle is dealing with.

♦ **Changing down gears:** gently apply the footbrake with your right foot to reduce the speed of the vehicle. At this point it is important to keep your right foot gently on the brake to control the vehicle. Use your left foot to push the clutch pedal firmly to the floor and then choose the gear you need. Once you have done this you may start releasing the clutch pedal slowly to engage the new gear. Once you have reached the speed you want and completed the gear change you may now release the footbrake as required and continue with use of the accelerator.

♦ **Changing up gears:** as you increase your speed you will also have to change gears. As you approach the speed at which a gear change is required remove the pressure of your right foot from the accelerator. Press the clutch pedal firmly to the floor and chose the gear you need. Once you have done this you may start releasing the clutch pedal slowly to engage the new gear. As you finish releasing the clutch pedal you may re-apply pressure to the accelerator with your right foot.

- As required, apply the handbrake after you have brought the vehicle to a full and complete stop.
- The handbrake is used to secure your vehicle on an incline or when stopped for a prolonged period in traffic. Use of the handbrake may not be required if stopping briefly on a surface where the vehicle will not roll.

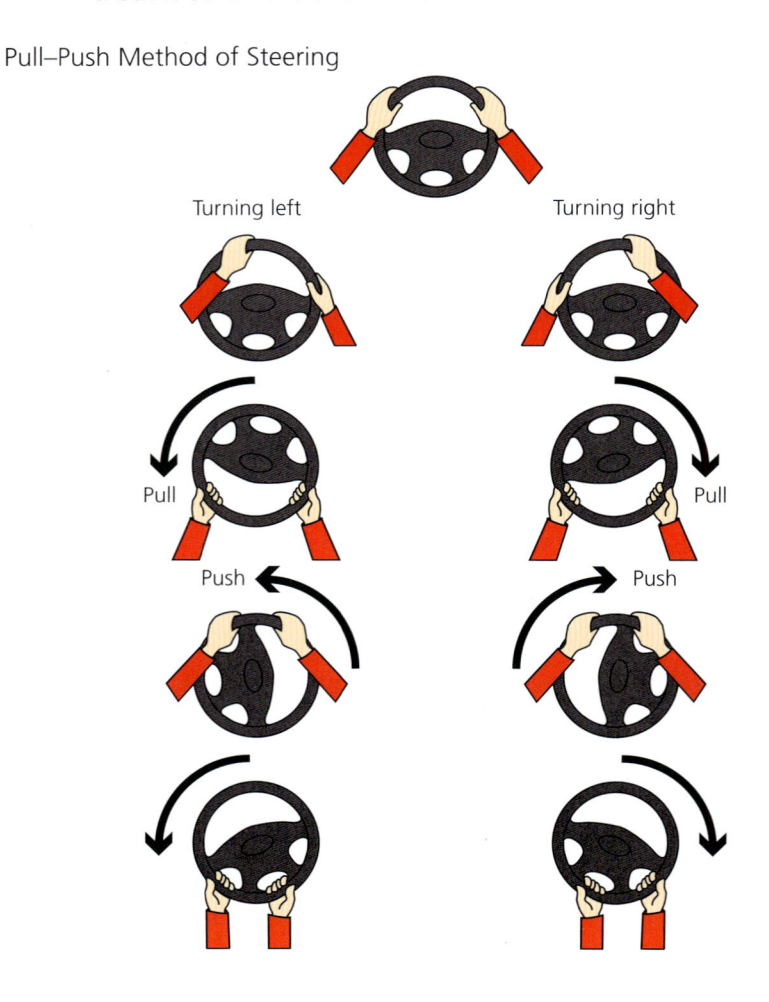

Pull–Push Method of Steering

Turning left

Turning right

Pull

Pull

Push

Push

Step-by-Step Breakdown of Tester's Report Form

- It is recommended that you use the pull–push method of steering. This is where both hands work together; the idea is that one hand pulls the wheel as the other hand pushes the wheel in the desired direction.
- Be confident about using your secondary controls when required as you are driving your vehicle. For example, know which controls to use to prevent condensation on the windows.

13. Speed

Excessive speed is seen as one of the biggest factors in road traffic accidents. You are expected to comply with speed limits. These limits are generally banded at 50 km/h, 60 km/h, 80 km/h, 100 km/h and 120 km/h on the motorway. Lower local limits may also be in place which you must obey.

Stopping Distances in Dry and Wet Conditions

Speed (km/h)	Reaction distance (m)	Braking distance (m)	Total stopping distance (m)	Speed (km/h)	Reaction distance (m)	Braking distance (m)	Total stopping distance (m)
30	5.5	5.3	10.8	30	5.5	9.4	14.9
50	9.2	14.8	24.0	50	9.2	26.1	35.2
60	11.0	21.4	32.4	60	11.0	37.5	48.5
80	14.7	38.0	52.7	80	14.7	66.7	81.4
100	18.3	59.4	77.7	100	18.3	104.3	122.6
120	22.0	85.5	107.5	120	22.0	150.2	172.2

Top Tips

- The speed limit shows the maximum allowable speed. A safe driver will also consider other factors such as road and weather conditions and reduce speed accordingly.
- You should reduce your speed if your visibility is reduced.
- In normal driving circumstances you should increase or reduce your speed smoothly.
- Note that speed limits may change frequently and must be obeyed accordingly.

14. Traffic Controls

All road markings, signs, pedestrian crossings, bus lanes, cycle lanes, Gardaí and school wardens must be obeyed and complied with.

Top Tips

- Do not enter a yellow box junction unless it is clear to exit without stopping. However, there is an important and useful exception. When turning right you may enter the yellow box junction and stop if necessary while waiting for a gap in oncoming traffic. Remember not to enter the yellow box if it would obstruct traffic that has the right of way.

Step-by-Step Breakdown of Tester's Report Form

Yellow Box Junction

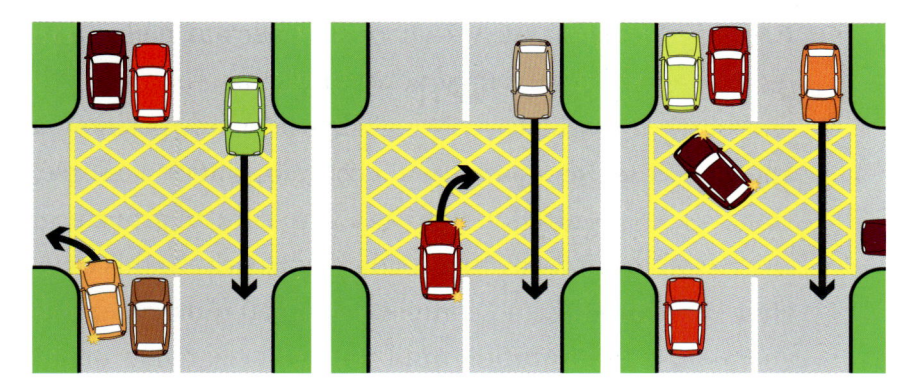

♦ Observe pedestrians who are close to zebra crossings and junctions. Be aware that pedestrians may cross the road and you may need to slow down or stop as required.

- Be aware that junctions may be controlled by a variety of traffic light types, such as filter arrows and pedestrian lights, and must be obeyed accordingly.
- Sometimes road signs/markings may be poorly positioned and you must negotiate them accordingly. For example, you may be required to stop at a stop sign in a position where you cannot see other road users clearly. In this case, after the initial full and complete stop you must creep out and observe with caution until you get a clear view of the road situation.

15. Right of Way

It is expected that you yield right of way to other road users (allow other road users to proceed) as required. Yielding right of way is required when moving off, turning, at junctions, overtaking, at roundabouts and changing lanes. You must also yield when required by road signs and markings.

Top Tips

- Sometimes junctions will be marked 'Géill Slí', or 'Yield' or 'Yield Right of Way'. These all have the same meaning and must be obeyed. It is wise to reduce your speed accordingly as you approach such junctions. Remember that a full and complete stop is not always necessary at a yield sign, as you may be able to proceed with caution if the way is safe.

Step-by-Step Breakdown of Tester's Report Form

♦ Yield right of way whenever you are reversing. This can be a particularly hazardous manoeuvre so listen and look for potential hazards from all directions.

♦ Junctions can sometimes be complex and you may be required to work in conjunction with other road users to negotiate a junction.

♦ Turning right at a crossroads can be a difficult where vehicles have equal ownership of the junction. This is normally dealt with by either turning back to back or near-side to near-side.

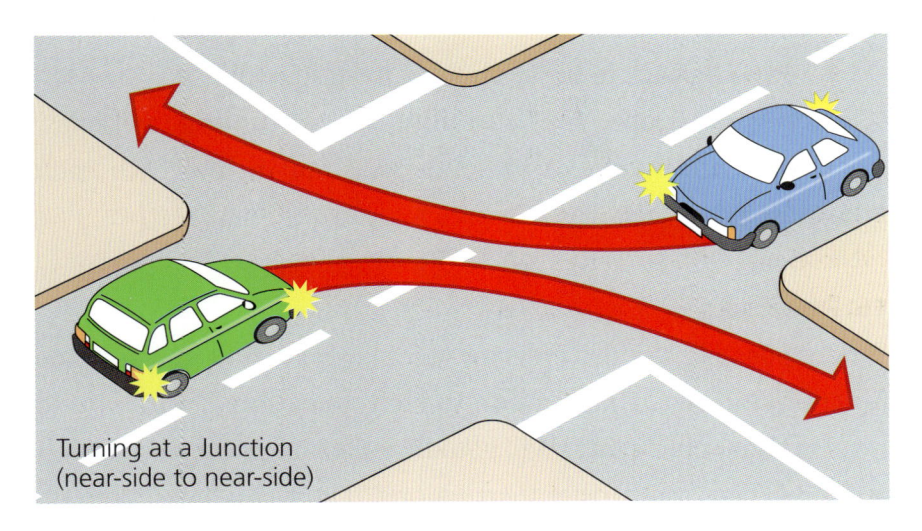

Turning at a Junction
(near-side to near-side)

♦ **Turning near-side to near-side:** This is where the two opposing vehicles start the turn while still facing each other. The turn is completed by either or both vehicles when it is safe to proceed.

43

Turning at a Junction
(back to back)

♦ **Turning back to back:** This is a technique that may be used to maximise the visibility of oncoming vehicles, particularly where junctions are not in line with each other.

16. Reverse

Where possible, the driver tester will ask you to pull in before the junction and say 'This road on the left is the one I want you to reverse your vehicle into. Will you drive past it and stop on the left and I will give you further instructions.' Once you have taken up your starting position for reversing the driver tester will say 'Reverse into this road on the left. You should continue reversing, while it is safe to do so, keeping reasonably close to the left. I'll tell you when you have gone back far enough. You may start when you are ready.'

Step-by-Step Breakdown of Tester's Report Form

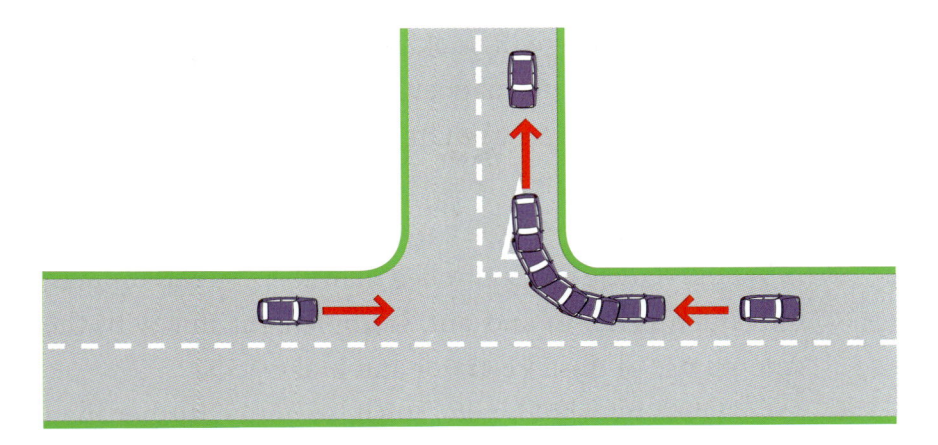

Reversing Left Around a Corner

Top Tips

- ♦ Get your starting position correct. In other words, park parallel to and within 18 inches (45 cm) of the kerb when putting your vehicle into position for reversing. Parking too close to the kerb or at an angle may cause the vehicle to drift too wide or too close to the kerb when reversing.
- ♦ Normally your reverse light(s) should come on once you place your vehicle into reverse gear. Use of your amber indicators is not usually required for the reverse manoeuvre.
- ♦ If another road user or pedestrian passes close to you during this manoeuvre you are required to slow down and yield right of way if required.
- ♦ Observation is not simply just looking where you are going. You must look and listen for other potential hazards that may come from any direction.

45

- The driver tester will look for a reasonable level of competence with this manoeuvre. For this reason you will be required to reverse until the tester requests you to stop (this is approximately three car lengths). Remember to yield to other road users.
- Move the vehicle in a controlled manner by gently dipping the clutch pedal in and out. Complement this with the smooth use of the accelerator and brake pedal.
- An ideal result would be to finish up not be further than 18 inches (45 cm) from the kerb. Avoid getting too close to the kerb as this will increase the risk of mounting the kerb and will also allow you less room for manoeuvring.
- Be advised that if you are being tested on category EB (vehicle drawing a trailer) you will be given a choice of performing a left- or right-hand reverse.

17. Turnabout

For this part of your test the driver tester will ask you to 'Turn your car around on the road to face the opposite way. You may go over and back more than once if necessary. You may start when you are ready.'

Top Tips

- Move your vehicle in a controlled manner, dipping the clutch in and out gently in conjunction with the appropriate use of the accelerator and brake pedal.

Step-by-Step Breakdown of Tester's Report Form

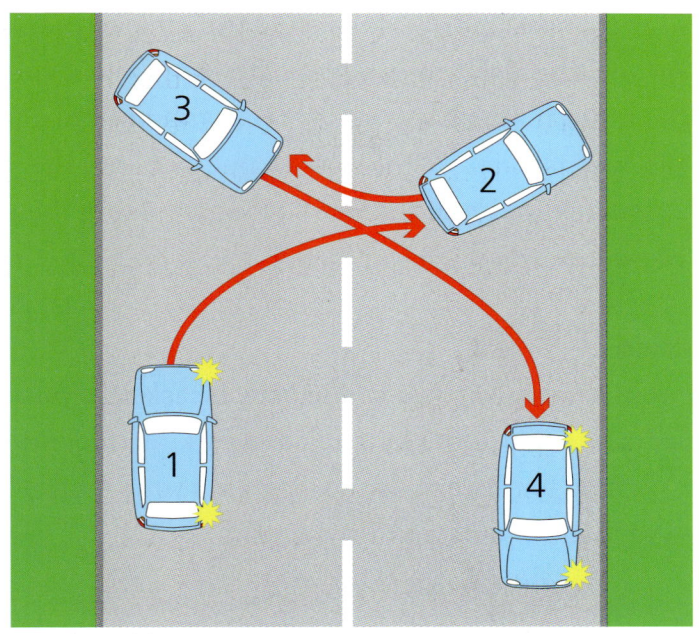

Turnabout Manoeuvre

- Avoid turning the steering wheel when the vehicle is stopped. In tight spaces turn the steering wheel relatively swiftly as you move your vehicle in a controlled manner.
- Be particularly aware that other road users may come along as you make this manoeuvre. Remember to yield right of way to other road users.
- If you are beckoned on by another road user, ensure that it is safe and appropriate for you to proceed before you take any action. Do not beckon other road users as you may invite them into a hazardous situation.
- Use your handbrake to hold your vehicle in place during

gear changes and also to prevent the vehicle from rolling.
- ♦ As you are about to complete the turnabout manoeuvre the tester may ask you to 'Proceed with normal driving if the way is safe.' If the way is not safe use the correct procedure and pull in. Move off again using the correct procedure when the way is safe.

18. Parking

During your driving test you will usually be asked to pull in and park your car a few times. I have divided parking into three basic types of parking for the test, namely parking your vehicle before, during and at the end of your driving test.

Top Tips

- ♦ Before your test it is essential to park your vehicle legally and not to cause obstruction. It is also wise to have the vehicle pointing with the flow of traffic or reversed into an available parking bay. The idea here is to keep the start of your driving test as simple as possible. Avoid putting your vehicle in a position where you will have to reverse out of a parking space or cross lanes to merge with the flow of traffic.
- ♦ During your driving test the driver tester will ask you to pull in and park beside a kerb. This often takes place on a hill or steep incline. This means you will have to secure the vehicle safely by applying the handbrake and engaging

Step-by-Step Breakdown of Tester's Report Form

neutral gear. You will then be asked to move off again (this is commonly called the hill start). The idea here is not only that you follow the correct MSMM (Mirror–Signal–Mirror–Manoeuvre) routine when moving off (remember to check your blind spots) but also that you prevent the vehicle from rolling backwards.

- As you come back to the test centre the driver tester will advise you to find a suitable place to park. Keep this as simple as possible by parking your vehicle legally and not making things over-complicated. In other words, choose the safest and most obvious legal parking space.

7 Sample Questions with Answers

Questions

Road Markings

1. When can you cross a continuous white line?
2. Where there is a continuous white line and a broken white line along the centre of the road, which line should be obeyed?
3. Are you allowed to park opposite a continuous white line?
4. What does a single broken white line mean?
5. What do two broken white lines along the centre of the road signify?
6. What do the zigzag lines on each side of a zebra crossing mean?

Road Procedure

7. What rules apply to a yellow box junction?
8. Who has priority at a junction of equal importance?
9. When can you overtake on the left-hand side or inside lane?
10. On what occasions should you give way to pedestrians?
11. Explain the two second rule?

Night-time Driving

12. When should you dip your headlights?
13. What should you do if dazzled by headlights?

Sample Questions with Answers

Parking Regulations
14. Where should you not park?
15. How far from a zebra or pedestrian crossing on a two-way street can you legally park?
16. How far from a zebra or pedestrian crossing on a one-way street can you legally park?
17. What does a double yellow line mean?
18. What does a single yellow line mean?

The Vehicle
19. What lights should your vehicle (car) be equipped with?
20. What is the minimum legal tread depth of a tyre for a standard vehicle?
21. What is the minimum legal tread depth of a tyre for a vintage vehicle or motorcycle?

Traffic Lights
22. What does a green filter arrow light mean?
23. What does a green light mean?
24. In what order do traffic lights change?
25. What does a flashing amber light at a pelican crossing mean?
26. You are approaching traffic lights and they change to amber; what is the required action?

Pelican and Zebra Crossings
27. What is the difference between a zebra and a pelican crossing?

28. How would you recognise a zebra crossing at night?
29. What do the white zigzag lines at a zebra crossing mean?
30. How should a pedestrian claim priority at a crossing?

Seat Belts
31. Who is exempt from wearing a safety belt?
32. Who is responsible for the wearing of safety belts of passengers under seventeen years of age?

Road Signs
33. What shape and colour are hazard warning signs?
34. What colour are regulatory signs?
35. What colour are motorway signs?
36. Identify the following road signs:

Sample Questions with Answers

Answers

Road Markings
1. In case of emergency and for access.
2. The line closest the driver.
3. No.
4. Do not cross unless it is safe to do so.
5. Alerts the driver to continuous white lines ahead.
6. No overtaking and no parking.

Road Procedure
7. Do not enter the yellow box junction unless it is clear to exit without stopping.

    Exception: When turning right you may enter the yellow box junction and stop if necessary while waiting for a gap in oncoming traffic. Remember not to enter the yellow box if it would obstruct traffic that has the right of way.
8. Traffic to your right.
9. You can overtake on the left-hand side or inside lane in the following situations:
    - When the driver in front has moved out and signalled their intention to turn right
    - When vehicles in the right-hand lane are moving more slowly than vehicles in the left-hand lane
    - When you are turning left yourself
10. You should give way to pedestrians:
    - When they are already crossing at a junction

- ❏ When they are on a zebra crossing
- ❏ When they are crossing at a pelican crossing where the light is red or flashing amber.
11. Leave a two second gap between you and the vehicle in front in normal driving conditions. Double this distance in wet conditions.

Night-time Driving

12. You should dip your headlights in the following situations:
    - ❏ When following close behind another vehicle
    - ❏ When meeting an oncoming vehicle
    - ❏ In built-up areas
    - ❏ At the beginning and end of lighting up times
    - ❏ In poor visibility, e.g. fog
    - ❏ In continuously lit areas
    - ❏ To avoid inconveniencing other road users
13. Slow down and stop in a safe place if necessary.

Parking Regulations

14. You should not park:
    - ❏ On zigzag lines
    - ❏ On double yellow lines
    - ❏ On cycle tracks
    - ❏ Within five metres of a junction
    - ❏ In areas marked as taxi ranks and bus stops
    - ❏ Along a single yellow line during business hours

❏ At any place where vision is restricted, e.g. the brow of a hill
15. Fifteen metres on the each side.
16. Fifteen metres on the approach side and five metres on the exit side.
17. Parking prohibited at all times.
18. You must not park here during the times shown.

The Vehicle
19. Your vehicle must be equipped with the following lights:
    ❏ Two headlights (white or yellow)
    ❏ Two white sidelights
    ❏ Front and rear direction indicator lights (amber only)
    ❏ Two red brake lights
    ❏ Two red lights (commonly known as tail lights)
    ❏ Two red reflectors
20. 1.6 mm.
21. 1 mm.

Traffic Lights
22. You may move in the direction of the arrow, assuming it is safe and the way is clear, even if a red light is also showing.
23. Go if the way is clear.
24. Red, green and amber.
25. You must yield to pedestrians.
26. Stop unless it is unsafe to do so.

Pelican and Zebra Crossings

27. A pelican crossing is controlled by lights; a zebra crossing is controlled by the presence of pedestrians.
28. Flashing amber beacons.
29. No overtaking and no parking.
30. By putting a foot on the road.

Seat Belts

31. Those who are exempt from wearing a safety belt include:
    - ❑ People who wear a disabled person's belt
    - ❑ Driver testers during a driving test
    - ❑ Driving instructors during a driving lesson
    - ❑ People who hold a certificate stating that they should not wear a belt on medical grounds
    - ❑ Gardaí in the course of their duty
    - ❑ Members of the Defence Forces in the course of their duty
32. The driver.

Road Signs

33. Diamond or rectangular in shape with a black border and black symbols or letters on a yellow background.
34. Red border and black symbols or letters on a white background.
35. White symbols or letters on a blue background.
36. Road signs are:

Sample Questions with Answers

(a) No entry
(b) Turn left ahead
(c) 120 km/h maximum speed limit (normally used on a motorway)
(d) Stop
(e) Level crossing ahead guarded by lights and lifting barriers
(f) Junction ahead with major road
(g) 200 m to end of motorway
(h) Contra flow bus lane

8 The Essential Top Ten Checklist to Pass the Test

1. Confirm time, date and location of your test with your correspondence from the RSA.
2. Make sure your permit is valid and in date.
3. Make sure your EDT logbook is fully completed and stamped by your ADI (RSA approved driving instructor).
4. Ensure your vehicle is reasonably clean and in a roadworthy condition. For example, tyres should be in good condition and lights in working order. Make sure there is plenty of fuel in your vehicle.
5. Check your vehicle discs are valid and in date, i.e. your insurance, tax and NCT (if required) discs should be visible and secured to the inside of the windscreen.
6. Have a thorough knowledge of the rules of the road and be able to identify and comply with all signs and road markings.
7. Be competent in the opening and closing of the bonnet and the identification of the engine's main components.
8. Be skilled in operating all the vehicle's secondary controls (for example, wipers, lights and ventilation).
9. Have an excellent knowledge of the driving test routes. Using the services of your local ADI is invaluable for this.
10. Ensure your 'L' plates are securely attached to the front and

rear of your vehicle. The official guideline is to have a rectangular plate or sign bearing the letter 'L' not less than fifteen centimetres high in red on a white background and with a border of at least 2 cm at the front and rear of your vehicle.

9 How to Apply for Your Theory and Practical Driving Tests

In order for you to receive your full Irish driver licence you need first to pass your theory test and then your practical test. In this chapter you will find the information you need to accomplish this.

Step 1: Booking Your Theory Test

Online
You can book your theory test at www.theorytest.ie.

By Post
You may also get an application form from driver theory test centres or your local motor taxation office. Complete the form and post it to:

Driver Theory Test
PO Box 788
Togher
Cork

Telephone and Fax

- You can call 1890 606 10 (lo-call rate) to book your theory test. This service is available Monday to Friday, 8.00 a.m. to 6.00 p.m. (excluding bank/public holidays).

How to Apply for Your Theory and Practical Driving Tests

- ❏ You can also text phone 1890 616 216 to book a theory test.
- ❏ To book via fax, fax the completed application form to 1890 606 906.

Note: Please have a credit/laser card and your PPSN (formerly RSI number) ready when booking your test.

Step 2: Booking Your Practical Test

Online
You may book your practical driving test at www.rsa.ie. If you are having problems applying for your test online you can contact the driving test section on 1890 406 040 (lo-call rate). This service is available Monday to Friday 9.15 p.m. to 5.30 p.m. (excluding bank/public holidays). You can also email DrivingTest@rsa.ie.

By Post
You may also get an application form from your local driving test centre or motor taxation office. Fill in the form and send it to:
Road Safety Authority
Driver Testing Section
Moy Valley Business Park
Primrose Hill
Dublin Road
Ballina
Co. Mayo

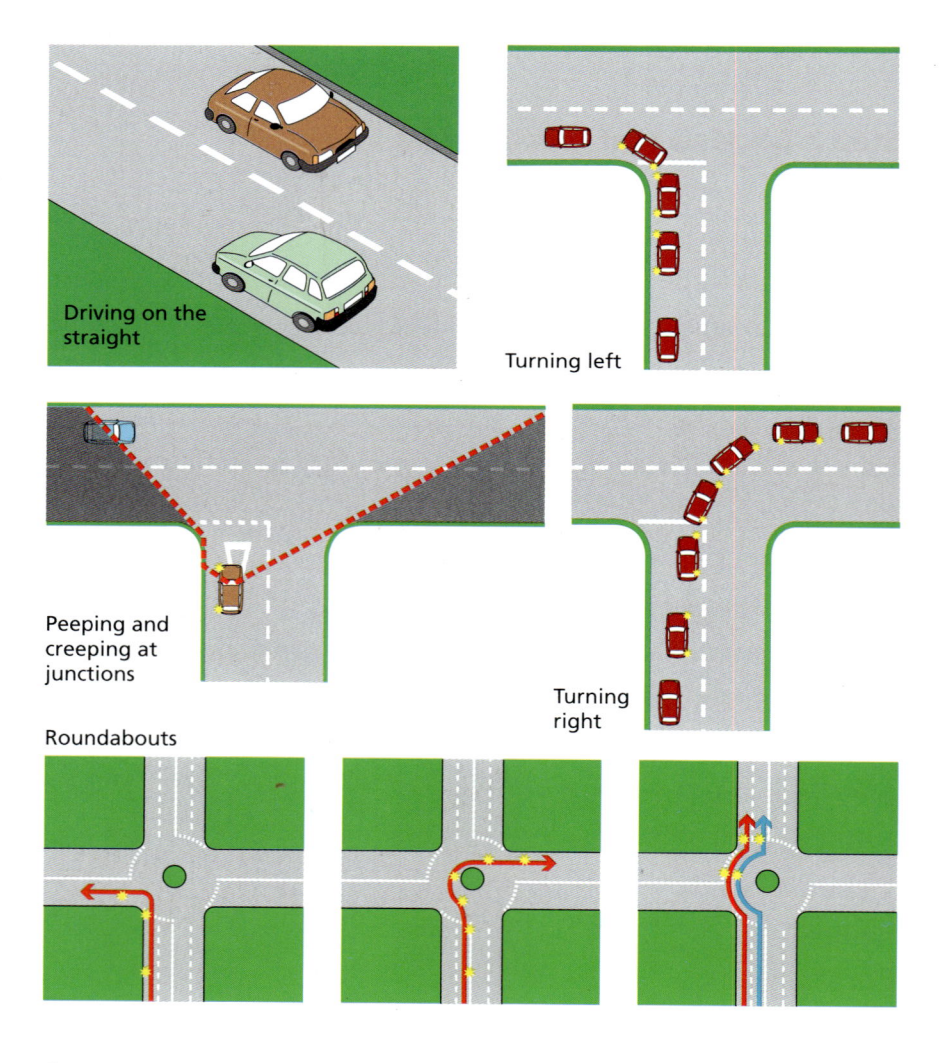

10 Illustrations of Vehicle Positions and Manoeuvres

Driving on the straight

Turning left

Peeping and creeping at junctions

Turning right

Roundabouts

62

Illustrations of Vehicle Positions and Manoeuvres

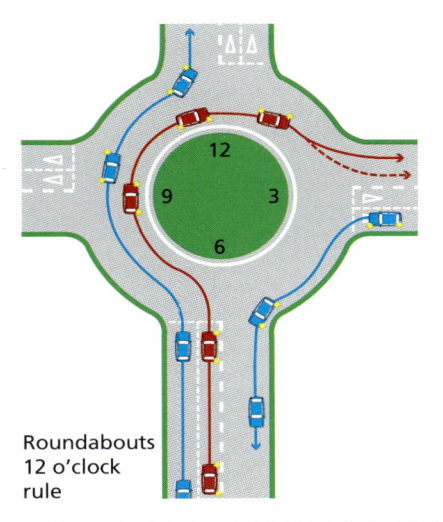

Hand signals for other road users behind you

FOR OTHER VEHICLES
I intend to turn right
(Arm out straight)

FOR OTHER VEHICLES
I intend to turn left
(Arm moves in anti-clockwise direction)

FOR OTHER VEHICLES
I intend to slow down
(Arm moves up and down)

Hand signals for a pointsman

FOR A POINTSMAN
I intend to turn right
(Arm out straight)

FOR A POINTSMAN
I intend to turn left
(Note that the car driver points the right forearm and hand with the fingers extended to the left)

FOR A POINTSMAN
I intend to go straight on
(Right arm is raised up)

Roundabouts 12 o'clock rule

Zebra crossings

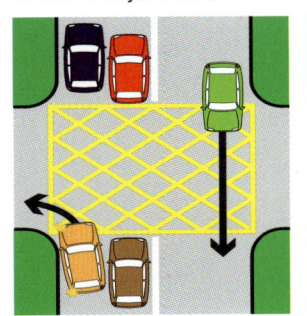

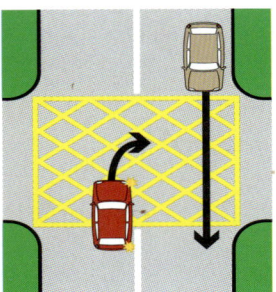

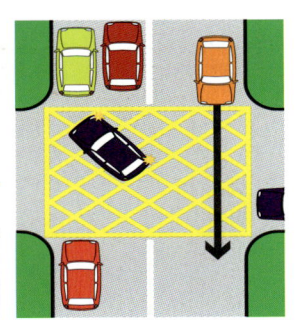

Yellow box junctions

63

Passing Your Driving Test in Ireland

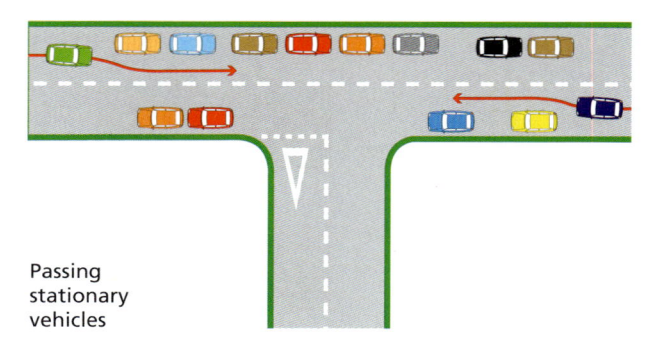

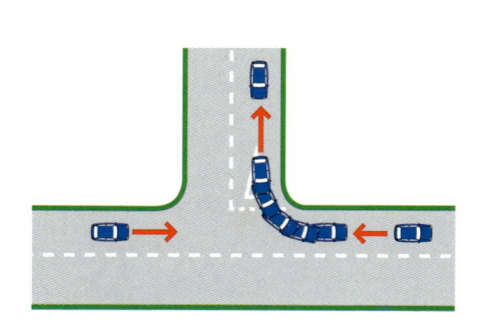

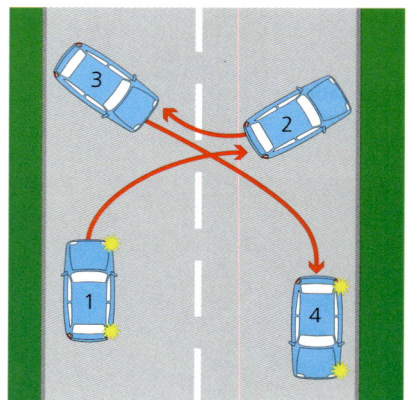

Passing stationary vehicles

Reverse left

Turnabout manoeuvre

Speed (km/h)	Reaction distance (m)	Braking distance (m)	Total stopping distance (m)	Speed (km/h)	Reaction distance (m)	Braking distance (m)	Total stopping distance (m)
30	5.5	5.3	10.8	30	5.5	9.4	14.9
50	9.2	14.8	24.0	50	9.2	26.1	35.2
60	11.0	21.4	32.4	60	11.0	37.5	48.5
80	14.7	38.0	52.7	80	14.7	66.7	81.4
100	18.3	59.4	77.7	100	18.3	104.3	122.6
120	22.0	85.5	107.5	120	22.0	150.2	172.2

Irish Road Signs

11

Regulatory Traffic Signs

Stop	Yield	Yield
School warden's stop sign	No left turn	No Entry
No right turn	Parking prohibited	Clearway
Max speed limit 30km/h	Max speed limit 50km/h	Max speed limit 60km/h

65

Passing Your Driving Test in Ireland

Max speed limit 80km/h   Max speed limit 100km/h   Max speed limit 120km/h

No overtaking   Taxi Rank

Parking permitted

Pedestrianised street →

Mandatory signs at junctions (white and blue)

Turn left ahead   Turn right ahead   Turn left   Turn right

Pass either side   Straight ahead   Keep right   Keep left

66

Irish Road Signs

With flow bus lane on left   With flow bus lane on right   Contra flow bus lane

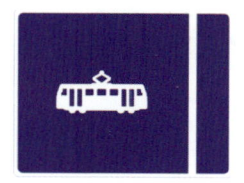

Tram lane on left   Tram lane on right

Start of cycle track   End of cycle track

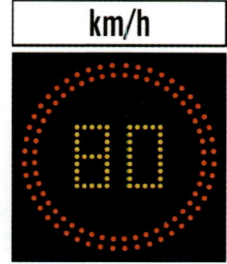

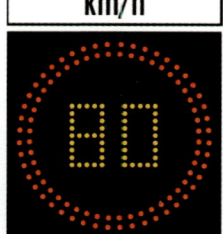

Electronic variable
speed limit sign (tunnel only)

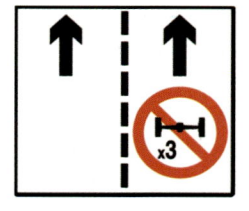

In a tunnel goods vehicles
cannot use right-hand lane
(by reference to number of axles)

67

Passing Your Driving Test in Ireland

Warning Traffic Signs

This section includes signs that warn road users of a hazard ahead. They are diamond or rectangular in shape and have a black border and black symbols or letters on a yellow background.

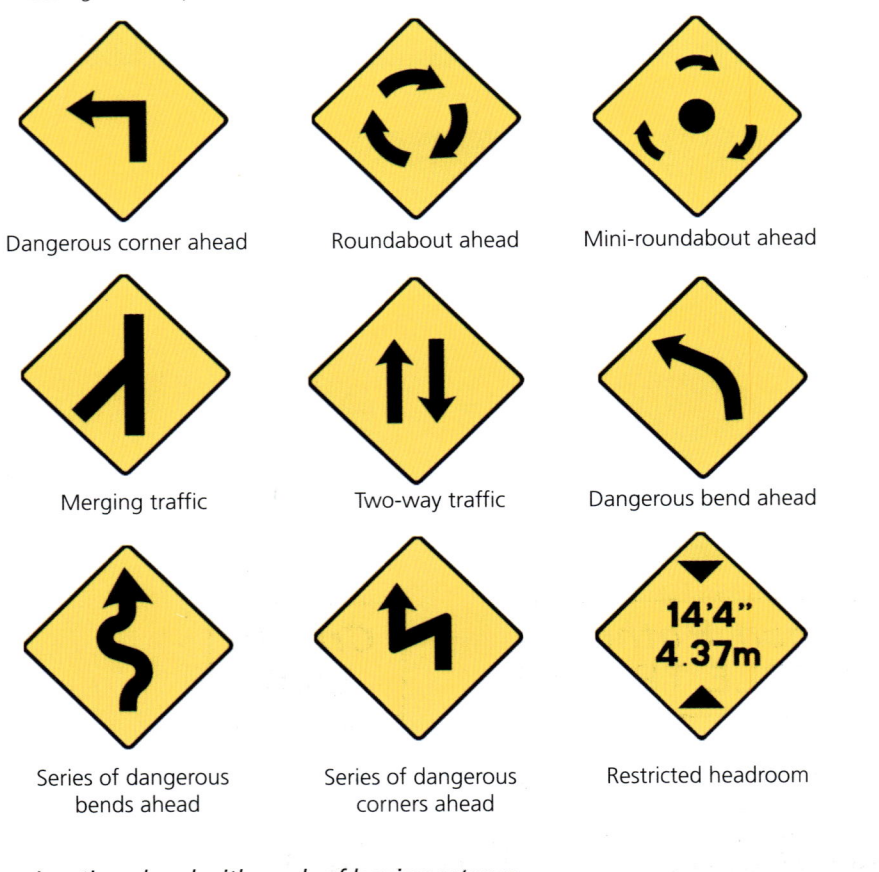

| Dangerous corner ahead | Roundabout ahead | Mini-roundabout ahead |

| Merging traffic | Two-way traffic | Dangerous bend ahead |

| Series of dangerous bends ahead | Series of dangerous corners ahead | Restricted headroom |

Junction ahead with roads of less importance (the latter being indicated by arms of lesser width)

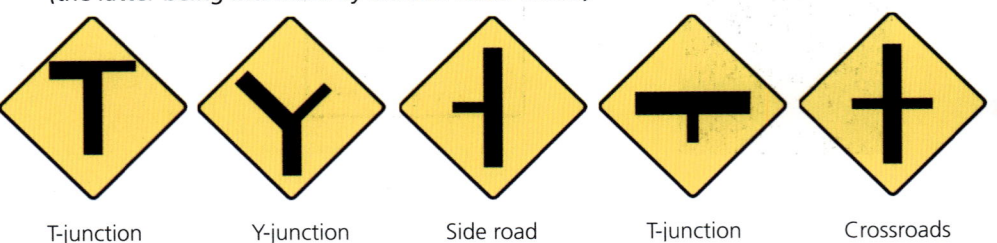

| T-junction | Y-junction | Side road | T-junction | Crossroads |

68

Irish Road Signs

Junction ahead with a road or roads of equal importance

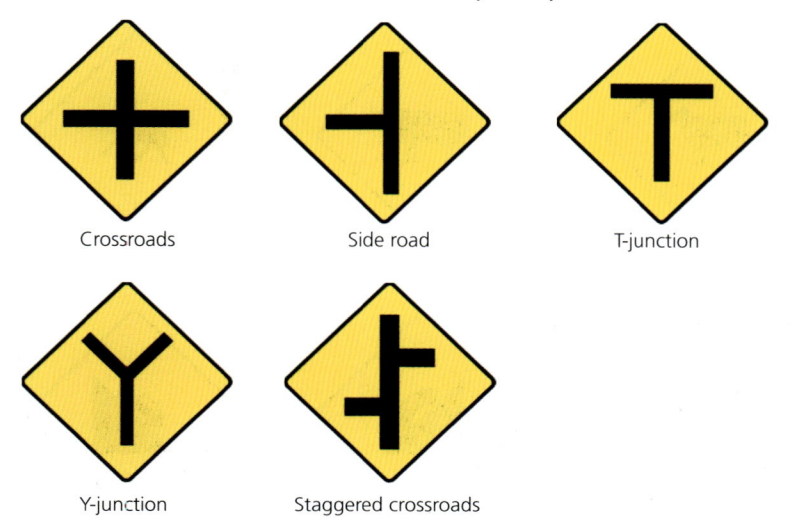

Crossroads

Side road

T-junction

Y-junction

Staggered crossroads

Advance warning of a major road (or dual carriageway ahead)

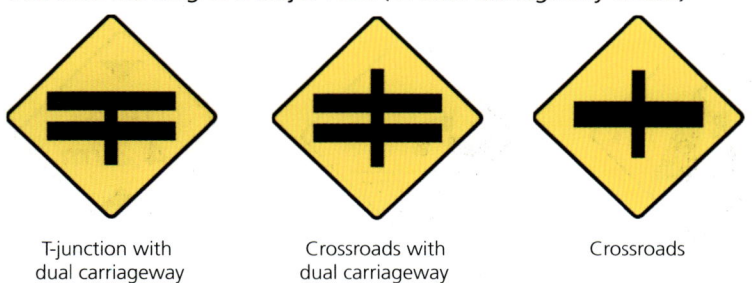

T-junction with dual carriageway

Crossroads with dual carriageway

Crossroads

General purpose warning signs

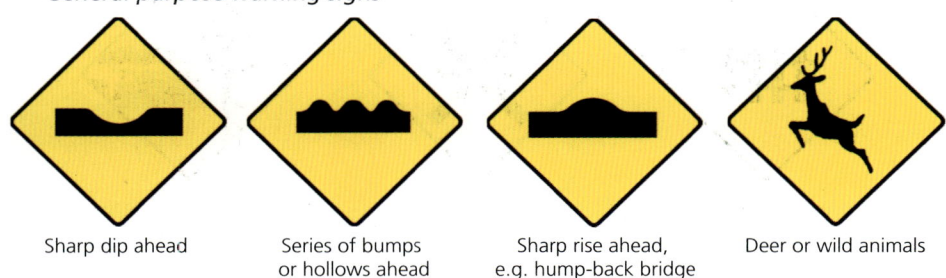

Sharp dip ahead

Series of bumps or hollows ahead

Sharp rise ahead, e.g. hump-back bridge

Deer or wild animals

Passing Your Driving Test in Ireland

General purpose warning signs

Sheep

Cattle and farm animals

Accompanied horses and ponies

Crosswinds

Steep descent ahead

Steep ascent ahead

Danger of falling rocks

Unprotected quay, canal or river ahead

Low bridge ahead (height restriction shown)

Level crossing ahead, guarded by gates or lifting barrier

Level crossing ahead, unguarded by gates or lifting barrier

Level crossing ahead with lights and barriers

Irish Road Signs

Warning signs for schools and children

School ahead

School children crossing ahead

Aire Leanaí

CAUTION CHILDREN

Children crossing (in residential area)

Warning Signs for Road Works

This section includes the warning signs for roadworks. Like other warning signs, these are diamond or rectangular in shape and have a black border and black symbols or text. However, they are orange in colour instead of yellow

Roadworks ahead

One-lane crossover (out)

One-lane crossover (back)

Move to left (one lane)

Move to right (one lane)

Move to left (two lanes)

Move to right (two lanes)

Obstruction between lanes

Passing Your Driving Test in Ireland

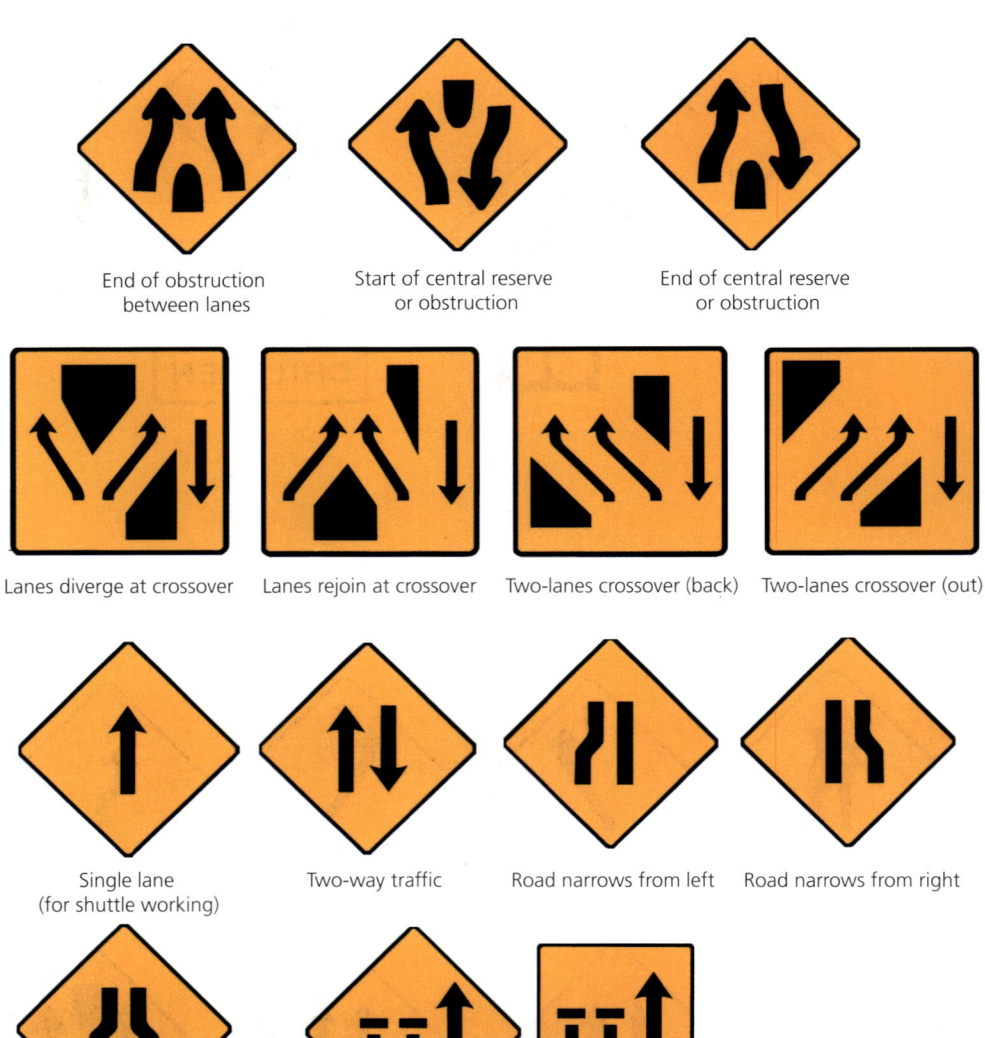

End of obstruction between lanes

Start of central reserve or obstruction

End of central reserve or obstruction

Lanes diverge at crossover

Lanes rejoin at crossover

Two-lanes crossover (back)

Two-lanes crossover (out)

Single lane (for shuttle working)

Two-way traffic

Road narrows from left

Road narrows from right

Road narrows on both sides

Two nearside lanes (of three) closed (two alternative styles)

Irish Road Signs

Offside lane (of four) closed	Nearside lane (of four) closed
Two offside lanes (of four) closed	Two nearside lanes (of four) closed
Side road on left	Side road on right
Site access on left	Site access on right
Temporary traffic signals ahead	Flagman ahead
Queues likely	Hump or ramp
Uneven surface	Slippery road
Loose chippings	Pedestrians cross to left

73

Passing Your Driving Test in Ireland

Pedestrians cross to right

Overhead electric cables

Motorway Signs

These signs are rectangular with blue backgrounds and white writing or symbols.

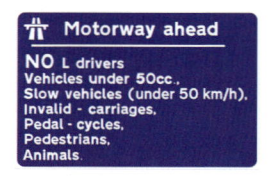

Motorway ahead
NO L drivers
Vehicles under 50cc.,
Slow vehicles (under 50 km/h),
Invalid - carriages,
Pedal - cycles,
Pedestrians,
Animals.

Motorway ahead

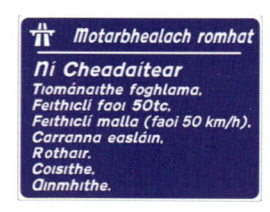

Motarbhealach romhat
Ní Cheadaítear
Tiománaithe foghlama,
Feithiclí faoi 50tc,
Feithiclí malla (faoi 50 km/h),
Carranna easláin,
Rothair,
Coisithe,
Ainmhithe.

Motorway ahead

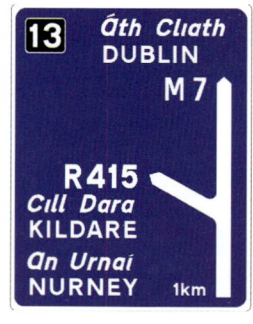

13 Áth Cliath
DUBLIN
M7
R415
Cill Dara
KILDARE
An Urnaí
NURNEY 1km

Advance direction sign

M7

Entry to motorway

300m to next exit

200m to next exit

100m to next exit

74

Irish Road Signs

Motorway ends 500m ahead    Motorway ends 1km ahead    End of motorway

Route confirmatory sign for M7

Advance direction sign for destination

Information Signs
This section includes road signs showing directions and the location of services or other places of interest to tourists.

Advance direction signs

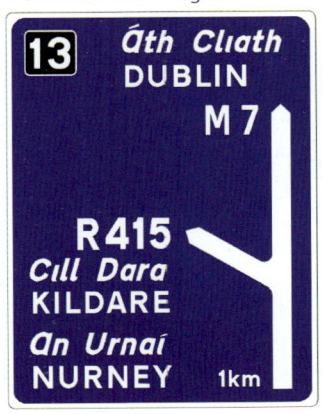

Motorway    National road   Regional road

National road

75

Tourist Information Signs

Tourist advanced direction sign

Advance direction to local services

Signing to approved tourist information

Pedestrian sign to a car park

Sign to approved tourist information point

Useful Websites

Department of Transport	www.transport.ie
Driving Test	www.drivingtest.ie
Driver Theory Test	www.theorytest.ie
An Garda Síochána	www.garda.ie
Irish Wheelchair Association	www.iwa.ie
National Car Test	www.ncts.ie
Penalty Points	www.penaltypoints.ie
Road Safety Authority	www.rsa.ie

Glossary of Frequently Used Terms

ADI: Approved Driving Instructor registered with the Road Safety Authority.

BLIND SPOT: This is an area than cannot be viewed directly by the road user or is visible in a mirror. It requires the road user to turn and look to see other road users who would not appear in direct view or in a mirror.

CATEGORY B VEHICLE: Four-wheeled vehicle with a gross weight not exceeding 3,500 kg. Passenger accommodation should not exceed eight people. The vehicle should be capable of a speed of at least 100 km/h. Typically, this is a car or light van.

COASTING: This is when the vehicle moves too freely. This is sometimes caused by the clutch pedal being held down for an extended period of time or travelling in neutral gear.

EDT: Essential Driver Training is a course for category B permit holders (cars and light vans). It consists of twelve one-hour lessons following the prescribed syllabus with an ADI. If the date of issue of your first learner permit is on or after 4 April 2011 you must complete the EDT course before you are permitted to take your full driving test. EDT is not required if your first learner permit was issued before 4 April 2011.

EDT LOGBOOK: Each EDT lesson must be written into a logbook which you can obtain from your ADI. It must be signed by both the instructor and learner driver. It must also be stamped by your ADI after each lesson. Your completed logbook must be produced to your tester before you sit the test.

GRADUATED DRIVER LICENSING (GDL): The GDL system consists of the six-month rule and completing the EDT programme, followed by successfully passing your practical driving test.

LEARNER PERMIT: After passing the theory test you will be entitled to apply for your permit. You must carry this permit with you when driving. When driving you must also be accompanied and supervised by a person who holds a current and valid full licence for over two years for the same category of vehicle.

LIGHTING-UP HOURS: This is defined as 30 minutes after sunset and 30 minutes before sunrise.

NCT CERTIFICATE: Confirms that the vehicle is in a roadworthy condition at the time the test was conducted and the expiry date on the certificate indicates the last date before the next test is due for the vehicle. If your vehicle requires an NCT disc ensure that it is visible and correctly secured to the front windscreen of your vehicle.

Glossary of Frequently Used Terms

Test Frequency of NCT

Age of Vehicle	Test Frequency
0–3 years	No test required
4–9 years	Every 2 years
10 years plus	Annually
Cars registered before 1 January 1980	No test required

SECONDARY CONTROLS: These controls allow the vehicle to be seen by other road users and also allow the occupants to see out of the vehicle. For example, light, wipers and demisters.

SIX-MONTH RULE: New learner permits must be held by the test candidate for at least six months before the driving test can be conducted.

STOP: The vehicle must be brought to a full and complete stop.

SWAN NECK: This can occur on a right-hand turn when the vehicle has travelled too far forward, past the correct turning point, and results in a bigger steering effort to get the vehicle back into the correct position to complete the turn.

TWO SECOND RULE: Leave a two second gap between you and the vehicle in front. Pick a point the vehicle in front is passing and say the phrase 'Only a fool breaks the two second rule.' If you are still saying the phrase as you pass the point you picked you are too close to the vehicle in front and need to pull back. Double this distance in wet conditions.

Glossary of Frequently Used Terms

VALID DISCS: This refers to the insurance, tax and NCT (if required) discs that should be visible and attached securely to the inside of your front windscreen. Please ensure that these are in date and relate correctly to your vehicle.

YIELD: Right of way must be given to other road users.